The Economi
the Vicke

The Economic Consequences of the Vickers Commission

Laurence J. Kotlikoff

Civitas: Institute for the Study of Civil Society
London

First Published July 2012

© Civitas 2012
55 Tufton Street
London SW1P 3QL

email: books@civitas.org.uk

ISBN 978-1-906837-42-6

Independence: Civitas: Institute for the Study of Civil Society is
a registered educational charity (No. 1085494) and a company
limited by guarantee (No. 04023541). Civitas is financed from a
variety of private sources to avoid over-reliance on any single
or small group of donors.

Typeset by
Civitas

Printed in Great Britain by
Berforts Group Ltd
Stevenage SG1 2BH

Contents

Figures

Author

Laurence J. Kotlikoff is a William Fairfield Warren Professor at Boston University, a Professor of Economics at Boston University, a Fellow of the American Academy of Arts and Sciences, a Fellow of the Econometric Society, a Research Associate of the National Bureau of Economic Research, President of Economic Security Planning, Inc., a company specialising in financial planning software, a columnist for Bloomberg, a columnist for Forbes and a blogger for *The Economist*.

Professor Kotlikoff received his BA in Economics from the University of Pennsylvania in 1973 and his PhD in Economics from Harvard University in 1977. His most recent books are *Jimmy Stewart Is Dead; Spend 'Til the End*, co-authored with Scott Burns; *The Healthcare Fix*; and *The Clash of Generations*, co-authored with Scott Burns.

Acknowledgements

Thanks are due to Peter Morris, Geoffrey Wood and Richard Munro for their exceptionally thoughtful and useful comments on a draft of this report; also to David Green for conceiving this study and shepherding its completion, and to Nick Cowen at Civitas for his help.

Foreword

The great financial crash of 2008 led to significant reforms intended to prevent the same thing happening again, but Professor Kotlikoff argues that measures such as the Dodd-Frank Act in the US do not overcome the fundamental flaws in modern banking. His solution is limited purpose banking, which he first described in his book *Jimmy Stewart is Dead* (2010). The aim is to: 'Limit banks to their legitimate purpose – connecting lenders to borrowers and savers to investors – and don't let them gamble.'

In *The Economic Consequences of the Vickers Commission* he has applied the same analysis to the proposals of the Independent Commission on Banking, chaired by Sir John Vickers. Professor Kotlikoff concludes that banks should function more like mutual funds.

Modern mutual funds have been functioning successfully for several decades in America and many people in the UK will be familiar with funds like Fidelity and Vanguard. The essential feature of mutual funds that Professor Kotlikoff wishes to harness is that individual investors can gamble knowingly with their own money, whereas the mutual fund itself can't gamble with customers' cash. An individual can, for example, invest £1,000 in an index fund that tracks the Japanese stock market. The investor hopes the index will go up, but takes the risk that it will go down. The mutual fund in this case is only an intermediary that receives money from investors and buys Japanese stocks. It is not supposed to use the money for any other purpose, let alone gamble it on high-risk derivatives. And yet our high-street banks have often taken customers deposits and invested them in extraordinarily risky instruments while customers believed their money was in safe hands.

Limited purpose banking does not try to eliminate risk, or even prevent people from taking the most extreme gambles. It says only that they must do so with their own money and at their own risk. And above all, no third party such as the government will come to their rescue. Risks are fine but not with other people's money, unless you tell them first.

Bank current accounts would become cash mutual funds, literally holding nothing but cash, effectively a system of 100% reserve banking for demand deposits. Customers would write cheques, make payments by debit card, use mobile phone apps or withdraw cash as normal. Other functions of the financial services industry, including insurance, would also be carried out by limited-purpose mutual funds.

Despite its radicalism, limited purpose banking received wide support when first put forward in 2010. Robert Lucas Jr, professor of economics at the University of Chicago, said that Professor Kotlikoff had made a 'coherent, and convincing case for Limited Purpose Banking'. Niall Ferguson, professor of business administration at Harvard Business School, said 'I was wholly persuaded by the case he makes for Limited Purpose Banking.' And Simon Johnson, professor of entrepreneurship at MIT Sloan and former chief economist at the IMF, said 'If we implement Professor Kotlikoff's ideas – or any close approximation – the US can continue to generate entrepreneurship, growth, and jobs, without repeatedly having to bail out our big banks. This is beyond appealing; it is compelling.'

If Professor Kotlikoff and his allies are right, in implementing the proposals of the Vickers Commission we have only taken the first few stumbling steps towards effective bank reform in the UK.

David G. Green

Executive Summary

The Vickers Commission: redeeming the status quo

The Independent British Banking Commission, or the Vickers Commission, was charged with keeping the British economy safe from another major failure of its banking system – a failure from which the UK economy is still reeling. Unfortunately, it's done nothing of the kind. Instead, the Commission, whose recommendations the British government is eagerly adopting, plays lip service to real reform. Worse yet, its proposals may make British banking riskier than ever.

This is a dangerous dereliction of duty. Scaled by its economy, the UK has the world's largest banking system, with bank assets totalling four times GDP. As a result, the magnitude of Britain's financial crisis, when measured by the absolute size of state intervention, was nearly as large as that in the US and the eurozone.

Millions of British workers and retirees who've lost their jobs, life savings or both can attest to the terrible havoc traditional banking can wreak on peoples' lives. Yet financial business as usual, albeit with new cosmetics, is the Commission's answer. Apparently, the British banks are not only too big to fail: they are also too big to cross.

Faith-based banking

The history of bank failures, whether culminating in nationalisations, shotgun weddings (reorganisations) or formal bankruptcies is a long and sorry record of promises that can't be kept. But unlike standard corporate bankruptcies, bank failures can produce far greater fallout for a simple reason. Banks do not only market financial products: they also make financial markets.

Markets, be they for apples or loans, constitute critical public goods. Public goods, by their nature, are fragile economic arrangements whose provision should not be jeopardised. The financial market, resulting from the interconnected and interdependent activities of banks, is particularly fragile. Yet the Vickers Commission, in an act of reckless economic endangerment, perpetuates faith-based, casino banking, permitting up to 33 to 1 leverage. In so doing, the Commission leaves the financial market where it found it – hanging by a thread.

Furthermore, the spectre of major bank failures concentrates private expectations on bad times, leading households and businesses to take the separate actions, i.e. reducing their purchases and firing workers, needed to make their worst nightmares come true.

The potential of financial collapse to severely damage the economy via what economists call *coordination failure* gives banks tremendous leverage over the public, permitting them to promise more than they can deliver, take the upside on risky bets and leave the downside for taxpayers to cover.

Opacity and leverage: the root causes of financial system collapse

The Vickers Report is marked principally by its omissions. In particular, it fails to discuss either the public goods-nature of banking and why this peculiar institution demands special regulation. Nor does it address the root causes of the financial crisis, namely opacity and leverage, which, in unison, make such a lethal financial brew.

Markets don't operate well in the dark. When people don't know for sure what they are buying, the slightest evidence of misrepresentation or fraud can trigger a run on – actually, a run away from — the product in question.

Take the 1982 Tylenol scare. A mere four bottles of Tylenol in Chicago drug stores were opened and laced with cyanide by a miscreant, who has yet to be apprehended. Within a few days, seven people had died.

The news of these deaths instantly rendered worthless 30,000,000 bottles of Tylenol located worldwide. To prevent a re-occurrence of such a run, Johnson & Johnson, Tylenol's manufacturer, decided to disclose, in a verifiable manner, the contents of its bottles. They did so by packaging new Tylenol in safety-sealed containers.

No such disclosure has occurred in banking. The world's premier secret-keepers, the banks, deem their proprietary information too valuable to disclose and their agents, the politicians, deem even the most rudimentary disclosure too costly to enforce. As a consequence, reported losses, suspicions of losses, or suspicions of suspicions of losses can spark bank runs, either quick and massive or slow and steady.

Those who run first are those bank creditors who have been induced to lend with the promise of quick escape if they smell something rotten. Moreover, the greater and shorter term the borrowing, the faster the run, since to the swift go the spoils. Thus leverage is not only the *sine qua non* for bank failure: it's also its catalyst.

The triumph of form over substance

Instead of fixing the real problems with banking – opacity and leverage – the Vickers Commission Report pretends to fix banking by re-arranging the deck chairs. Specifically, the Commission proposes 'ringfencing' retail banking by separating the 'good' bits of banking from the 'bad' bits, while leaving all the bits under the same roof.

Good banks, to be owned and operated by bad banks, will only hold good assets (e.g. 'safe' mortgages and sovereign bonds), have only good customers (e.g. retail depositors and small and medium sized enterprises), hold a bit more capital, and do only good things (i.e. no proprietary trading or transacting in derivatives). The good banks will also be closely monitored by the government and be bailed out as needed.

The bad banks are the investment banks and other shadow and shadowy financial corporations. Bad banks will have bad customers, namely large corporations, foreigners and other bad banks. They will hold bad assets, like derivatives, engage in bad practices, like proprietary trading, hold a bit more capital, and have no formal right to government rescue.

Both good and bad banks will hold more capital against 'risky' assets, submit to stress tests, and make their longer-term debt loss-absorbing to speed up financial funerals (resolutions).

Good assets and good banks go bad

One glance at the current Eurozone crisis shows the folly of the Commissioners' way. Good/safe, AAA-rated assets, like Italian government bonds, can suddenly turn bad/risky.

Indeed, today's safest assets are, according to the market, UK gilts and US Treasuries. But based on long-term fiscal gap analysis, they are among the riskiest assets in the world. Yet, the Commission would allow good, ringfenced banks, to borrow 25 pounds for every pound of equity and invest it all in gilts. In this case, the Commission's ringfenced banks would fail if gilt prices dropped by just four per cent.

The fallacious rating and misjudgement of risk is one of the hallmarks of the financial crisis. In the months before they failed, both AIG and Lehman Brother bonds were rated AAA, as were trillions of dollars in top-tranched subprime collateralised debt obligations. Had the Commission's desired ringfenced banks been in existence, and had they purchased these 'safe' assets, they would surely have gone under.

Nor would the Commission's higher capital requirements have saved the day. These requirements are lower than Lehman's capital levels at the time it went under!

When trust takes a holiday, creditors don't find much comfort in capital ratios, and for good reason. The banks' opacity makes it virtually impossible to verify if their capital ratios are actually as high as advertised.

Bad banks are too big to fail

The Commission intimates that the bad banks won't be saved if they begin to fail. But the fact that it can't even bring itself to say so in plain English makes clear that this is a prayer, not a realistic implication of their reform.

In fact, the Commissioners have seen this movie. Lehman Brothers failure tested the proposition that big bad banks can fail. It failed. Lehman's failure set off such a massive run and freezing of the financial system that the US government made clear it would never permit another large financial company to go under. The Bank of England's intervention in Northern Rock and other UK financial companies provides further proof that bad banks will be saved in the final analysis.

Indeed, in pushing the proposition that bad British banks will be left to sink or swim, the Commission may have dramatically raised the risk of financial collapse in times of financial crisis. The reason is that if the bad banks' bad customers actually believe the Commission's intimations that their credits with the bad banks won't be honoured, they will exit stage left at the first sign of trouble. As a result, the instability of the bad banks and the entire financial system will increase.

In sum, the Vickers Report protects neither the good banks nor the bad banks. Nor does it protect the public from the failure of opaque, leveraged banking.

The solution: Limited Purpose Banking

Fortunately, there is a bold, meaningful reform to fix Lombard Street. But it's one the Commission essentially ignored, notwithstanding its strong endorsement by leading policymakers, economists and financial experts. The reform is called Limited Purpose Banking (LPB). It replaces 'trust me' banking with 'show me' banking:

- **LPB bans all limited liability financial companies from marketing anything but mutual funds.** Mutual funds, whether open-end or closed-end, are not allowed to borrow, explicitly or implicitly, and, thus, can never fail.

- **LPB uses cash mutual funds (replacing retail deposit accounts), which are permitted to hold only cash (currency), for the payment system.** Cash mutual funds are backed pound-for-pound by cash in the vaults and none of this cash is ever lent out.

- **LPB uses tontine-type mutual funds to allocate idiosyncratic risk,** be it mortality risk, longevity risk or commercial risk. And LPB uses parimutuel mutual funds to allocate aggregate risk. Its fully collateralised betting provides a completely safe way to provide CDSs, options, and other derivatives.

- **LPB mandates full and real-time disclosure.** It empowers the Financial Services Authority (FSA) to hire private companies working only for it to verify, appraise, rate and disclose, in real time, all securities held by mutual funds.

- **LPB requires mutual funds to buy and sell their securities in public auction markets to ensure the public gets the best price for its paper.**

Limited Purpose Banking's cash mutual funds would provide a perfectly safe payment system. These cash mutual funds would be the only mutual funds backed to the pound. All other mutual funds, be they closed- or open-end, would fluctuate in price. Since the mutual funds under Limited Purpose Banking hold no debt, neither they, individually, nor the financial system in its entirety, can fail. Large private losses could still take place within the financial system, but without endangering the rest of the economy or making claims on taxpayers.

Introduction

The United Kingdom is still reeling from the great financial crash. Real GDP remains below its 2007 level; the nation's 8.4 per cent unemployment rate is at a 16-year high; and youth unemployment is over 20 per cent.[1] Over three million Britons can't find work or have given up looking. Millions more are short on work – working part time or in jobs below, if not far below, their skill levels.

The crash and its recession have not only taken a huge toll on people's lives and the economy's performance. They've also devastated the government's finances. UK debt is now 65 per cent of GDP – twice the value a decade back. Notwithstanding major and, in some cases, draconian cuts in government social services, the UK deficit is still running close to 10 per cent of GDP.

This picture is bleak enough, but there are signs the country is again slipping into recession, with negative growth recorded in the last quarter of 2011 and first quarter of 2012. Back-to-back recessions, fairly close together, is economics' working definition of economic stagnation, if not depression.

Britain has the world's largest banking system when measured relative to the size of its economy. UK bank assets exceed GDP by a factor of four. The German and Irish factors are three, whereas the US factor is one.[2] Hence, the UK was particularly vulnerable to financial crises, let alone what Bank of England Governor, Mervyn King, called '…the most serious financial crisis we've seen, at least since the 1930s, if not ever'.[3] Indeed, thanks to the size of its banking sector, the absolute magnitude of Britain's financial bailout in the recent financial crisis was almost as large as those in the US and the eurozone.[4]

To insulate the economy from future financial crises, the Chancellor of the Exchequer established the Independent Commission on Banking, dubbed the Vickers Commission after its chairman, Sir John Vickers. The Commission's other members were Clare Spottiswoode, Martin Taylor, Bill Winters and Martin Wolf.

The Commission was charged with proposing structural and non-structural banking reforms to foster financial stability and competition. In April 2011, the Commission issued an interim report. It issued its final report in September 2011. The Commission's main proposals are to (a) ring-fence retail banking, (b) improve the ability of banks to absorb losses, and (c) enhance competition among banks.

HM Treasury indicated in December 2011 that it agreed with the Commission's recommendations and would produce a white paper in the Spring of 2012 laying out how it intends to implement the Vickers Commission's recommendations, albeit gradually, with full implementation to take eight years.

My object here is to review the Vickers Report. Were I to accept the report's unstated premises – that leveraged, opaque, complex, 'trust-me' banking is economically vital and can be made safe – my task would be both easy and dull. The report is over 200 pages, single-spaced. One could easily devote a large number of words to debating its details. But such an endeavour would be of little value as there is no clear basis to criticise reasonable judgments of practical experts on the narrow issue of how best to implement mistaken directives.

In fact, leveraged, opaque, complex banking is not economically vital. Nor can it be made safe by adopting the Commission's proposals or any close variant of them. The proposals represent timid tweaks of questionable feasibility to a financial system that has failed and will fail again, for two reasons.

First, the financial system is built to self-destruct. Indeed, the canonical economics model of fractional reserve banking, the Diamond-Dybvig model, demonstrates that 'trust-me banking' rests on collective belief that one's money is safe – a belief that can change, has changed, and will change on a dime. When that belief changes, it spells bank runs and economic distress, if not economic ruin. This knife-edge propensity of opaque, leveraged banking to flip from financial stability to financial collapse – what economists call *multiple equilibria* – is one of many reasons Bank of England Governor Mervyn King described the financial system's design as 'the worst possible'.[5]

Second, the financial system is virtually built for hucksters, with limited liability, leverage, off-balance sheet book-keeping, insider-rating, kick-back accounting, sales-driven bonuses, loss-driven bonuses (i.e. corporate theft), nondisclosure, director sweetheart deals, government bailouts and fraudulent security initiation. Hucksters make the system even more fragile because their behaviour, as much as poor investment returns, can induce financial panic when recovery of one's invested money is based on 'first-come, first-served'.

The report not only takes our built-to-fail financial structure as immutable. It also assumes that the same people that just undermined the system, facing the same incentives, will act in a responsible, trustworthy manner or be subject to more vigilant regulation by regulators who just proved their incompetence. Would this were so and would that the Commission had spared a few words to discuss this lovely prayer. But here and elsewhere, what most distinguishes the content of the Commission's report is its lack of content. It takes fabulously fragile, faith-based banking as God-given and ruffles as few banker feathers as possible.

In contesting the report's unsupported and unquestioned presumptions as well as its grievous omissions, I start by asking what's so special about the financial system that it (a) can cripple the economy and wreak havoc with the lives of millions of workers and retirees, (b) requires an army of regulators to oversee, and (c) necessitates one financial reform after another to 'fix' its behaviour.

Next I wonder why financial crises can be economically so deadly. Is it the breakdown of the payment system on which the report obsesses? Or is it something deeper and much more difficult to fix with measures geared to preserve the financial status quo?

This questioning would be of small practical value were banking, as we've known it, our only option and patching up traditional banking our only recourse. But there is a clear alternative, namely Limited Purpose Banking (LPB), which can make banking perfectly safe. LPB is 'show-me' banking. It features 100 per cent equity finance and full transparency, relegating leveraged, opaque, complex banking to financial companies willing to operate with unlimited liability. Its presentation permits a stark comparison between what the Commission wrought and what the United Kingdom, the US and other countries so desperately need.

The report devoted only seven of its hundreds of thousands of sentences to reviewing Limited Purpose Banking. Remarkably, these sentences badly mischaracterise the proposal and completely misstate its likely impacts. The concision of these misstatements tells us two things. First, the Commission felt no compulsion to ask big questions about the financial system, which an accurate and full discussion of LPB would have necessitated. Second, the Commission wanted to dismiss major alternatives to its policy prescription so as to focus attention solely on its preferred reform and limit questions to the details of implementation.

Presenting the public with a thick, highly detailed document that says: 'Do W. Doing anything but W is not worth even two paragraphs of consideration, and here's all the details for how to do W' naturally focuses attention on W and how to implement it. Government officials, on receipt of such a hefty financial repair book, presented, as it was, by a highly august body, could be counted on to accept the report's unstated premises and to delve immediately into its weeds. The Commission faced little risk that officials would react by saying: 'Sorry, this study is distinguished primarily by what's excluded. You ignored options X, Y and Z. Go back to work.'

Given my authorship of Limited Purpose Banking,[6] it will be tempting to dismiss my critique of the Vickers Report as self-serving. But ignoring this clear answer and discussing the report as if W were, in fact, the only appropriate reform would be a further disservice to the public. I also venture that the public, if not the bankers, will find it very hard to judge LPB as wanting in relation to the Commission's proposal.

This endeavour to contrast a real cure with a dangerous elixir would be a lonely venture were there not such a significant collection of prominent supporters of Limited Purpose Banking. This list includes a former US Treasury Secretary, a former US Secretary of Labor, seven Nobel Laureates in Economics, two former Chairmen of the President's Council of Economic Advisors, and a who's who of prominent finance specialists.*

Having disclosed my destination, let me clarify the route. I'll start by asking what's so special about banks that they must be repeatedly coddled, protected, defended, excused and rescued no matter the cost to the public purse. Once I've shown why the banks can bank on their protection money, I'll be in a position to show both that the Vickers Report ignored these problems and that Limited Purpose Banking can resolve them. After so doing, I'll examine the report in some detail starting with its views of LPB.

---

* The endorsements of *Jimmy Stewart Is Dead* document much of this support.

1. Why Is Banking Special?

Banks, and financial intermediaries in general, make markets. In making markets, they are very different from ordinary firms that simply produce goods for sale. Individual wheat farmers, for example, are not responsible for making sure that the wheat market operates. That's the business of a separate set of firms that broker between suppliers of and demanders for wheat and, in the process, clear the market. Banks broker between suppliers of funds and demanders for funds. In so doing, they help set the terms under which funds are supplied and demanded.

As market makers, banks are involved in the provision of a public good; i.e. markets, themselves, are public goods. Public goods come in many forms and vary greatly in their degrees of publicness. But in their purest version, public goods are completely non-rival and non-excludable in their use/consumption. Non-rival means that any number of people can simultaneously consume (enjoy the services of) the public good, and non-excludable means that no one can be kept from consuming (enjoying the services of) the public good.

A missile defence system is a good example. Increasing the size of the population doesn't diminish the system's ability to protect the existing population, i.e. everyone can fully enjoy all of the system's protection and any one person's benefit does not infringe on anyone else's. Nor can anyone be excluded from the system's protection.

A local road system, at least during periods without congestion, is another example of a 'pure' public good. More people can use the roads without encumbering their use by others, and there is no way to exclude access to the roads.

Markets have these features too. Adding more participants to a market does not lessen the market's value to existing participants. Indeed, the more participants, the

1

better. Thicker markets make for quicker sales and purchases at prices that are more reliable. And once a market is established, it's generally hard to keep anyone out.

Take trade fairs, which were held in the Middle Ages. These markets coordinated the meeting of buyers and sellers and could generally accommodate more participants at no impairment to the market's operation. Moreover, depending on the physical location/arrangement of the fair, it was hard to exclude participation.

The modern trade fair is the downtown business district and the suburban mall. These public goods facilitate trade in a variety of products, offer free access, and, except during holidays, operate with excess capacity in terms of being able to handle more customers at no cost to any shoppers.

But bringing together sellers and buyers is not sufficient to make a market. Purchase and sale arrangements have to be enforceable. Otherwise, no one would come to market. Hence one needs another public good, the constabulary, to enforce property rights and transference arrangements. And to overcome the inefficiencies of barter, yet another public good – a common currency – is needed to effect transactions. Note that the greater the number of people using a currency, the more valuable it becomes to those already using it. Furthermore, no one can be barred from swapping goods for currency.

The challenge in providing public goods

Because of their unique non-rivalness and non-excludability properties, the provision of public goods is never straightforward. Left to our own devices, none of us would build a missile defence system on our own. Instead, we'd all sit back and hope our neighbour would build one that would benefit us for free. Overcoming this *free-rider problem* requires organising and maintaining a government to provide the public good, with all the coordination difficulties that entails.

2

Trade fairs were susceptible to such 'You-first!' coordination problems. A trade fair could run aground if (a) everyone decided not to go because they believed no one else was going or (b) too many towns scheduled a fair at the same time of year, leaving everyone unsure where everyone else was going. The great trade fairs of Champagne in the twelfth and thirteenth centuries came to an end, in large part, because of the initiation of new fairs in Bruges, Cologne, Frankfurt, Geneva and Lyon. Similarly, downtown business districts have been killed by new malls, and new malls have been killed by newer malls. And sometimes new malls have killed not only business districts and old malls, but themselves as well.

In the case of money, having lots of circulating currencies runs the risk of people changing their beliefs about what currencies will retain purchasing power, instantly rendering suspect currencies less valuable, and, in the extreme, worthless.*

The fragility of traditional banking

The delicate nature of public goods makes traditional banking a very fragile institution. If banks fail, they not only take themselves down. They also limit the ability of people to engage in financial trade, i.e. they bring down the financial market itself. Even the failure of a single bank has the potential to greatly undermine the financial exchange system.†

---

* Yes, currency issuers may attempt to restore their currency's purchasing power by reducing supply, but doing so requires having 'hard' currency to spend on buying up their own weak currency.

† In defending their industry against regulation, bankers conveniently forget that they are running a market and argue that their industry is no different from any other. But when they get into trouble, they immediately run to the state claiming their failure will destroy the market.

3

The reasons are twofold. First, banks borrow from and lend to one another. Consequently, bank A's failure can initiate bank B's failure, which can initiate Bank C's, etc. Why? Because when A fails it may not be able to repay B, leading B to fail, which then is unable to repay C, leading C to fail, and so on.

Second, when banks exercise their 'right' to proprietary information, leaving their creditors in the dark as to precisely what they own and owe, the unexpected failure, near failure, or simply report of large losses of one bank can change the expectations of creditors about the solvency of other banks, who may hold similar assets or have incurred similar liabilities.

This can lead to a run on banks in which every channel through which banks borrow – inter-bank borrowing, issuance of demand deposits, creation of short-term saving accounts, sale of certificates of deposits, sale of medium- and long-term bank bonds, sales of convertible bonds, etc. – dries up.

The prototypical bank run by retail depositors, depicted so graphically in the Christmas movie, *It's a Wonderful Life*, which starred Jimmy Stewart as the thoroughly honest banker who comes under suspicion, is much less common these days thanks to retail deposit insurance. But that doesn't mean bank runs are a thing of the past. On the contrary, in the last four years, bank runs have become commonplace.

The freezing up of US credit markets, in the immediate aftermath of Lehman Brothers' collapse in September 2008, constituted a colossal run on US banks by creditors, other than retail depositors. Iceland, Ireland, Switzerland, the UK, Holland and other countries experienced similar non-insured creditor runs in 2007 and 2008 as their major banks ran aground. And during the entire life of the Commission and in the period since the issuance of its report, we've seen a massive bank run by non-insured creditors on banks in the eurozone that hold Portuguese, Irish, Italian, Greek and Spanish government bonds. Sophisticated insured depositors, who realize that the governments insuring their deposits don't have the means to do so, are also moving their money to Switzerland, German, the US and other safer havens.

These ongoing bank runs are the equivalent of suppliers not showing up at a trade fair because they can't trust demanders will pay for what they buy. In the case of a creditor run, the would-be creditors are the suppliers of funds who suddenly decide that the banks have lined up a set of demanders for their funds, be they mortgage borrowers, real estate investors, small business borrowers or large corporate borrowers, who may not be able to make good on their promises.

This will particularly be the case if creditors believe other creditors have the same view or will have the same view of those demanding credit. No creditor wants to be first to lend money if (a) the borrower's repayment depends on her ability to secure additional loans and (b) recourse to requisite additional funding is uncertain.

Since demand deposits are used to effect payments, bank runs by retail depositors is of central concern for maintaining a well-functioning payment system. But runs by retail depositors have not been the hallmark of the financial crisis. Indeed, the run by depositors on Northern Rock in September 2007 was the first such run by depositors on a British bank since 1866.[7] And it lasted just three days, at which point it was quelled by the British government's announcement that it was insuring all deposits. The US experienced no retail deposit runs whatsoever during the financial crisis, thanks, no doubt, to the Federal Deposit Insurance Corporation's decision to raise its insurance coverage from $100,000 to $250,000 per account.

From banking panic to economy-wide panic

The difficulty of coordinating economic activity – of getting the fragile public good known as the market to operate well – is hardly confined to the banking sector. Suppliers have to seek out demanders and demanders have to find suppliers for every product being bought and sold. As Keynes vigorously stressed, the state of business sentiment – what he called *animal spirits* – can make all the difference to whether an economy performs well or poorly, i.e. whether individual suppliers and demanders each take the costly and risky steps to find each other.

In 2009, Peter Diamond won the Nobel Prize in economics for his seminal 1982 paper entitled 'Aggregate Demand Management in Search Equilibrium',[8] which shows in the simplest possible context that, if economic agents expect bad times, they may each take self-interested steps that, taken together, ensure that bad times arise. By contrast, if they expect good times, their individual actions will produce that collective outcome.

Hence, when President Roosevelt proclaimed, at the height of the Great Depression, 'The only thing to fear is fear itself', he was dead on. What Roosevelt didn't need to stress, given the prevailing circumstances, was that collective fear, panic and pessimism can be economically deadly and can last for an incredibly long time.

In this regard, a large-scale banking crisis, whether marked by depositor runs, non-depositor creditor runs, bank failures, bank reorganisations, bank mergers (also known as 'shotgun weddings'), bank nationalisations or bank rescues, can produce a *coordination* failure, flipping the economy from a *good equilibrium* to a *bad equilibrium*. It can do so simply by changing expectations. A bad equilibrium is one in which small, medium and large employers fire or at least hold off hiring because they think (a) 'times are bad' (b) 'other companies are firing' and (c) 'we'll shortly have fewer customers'.

In September 2008 when, in the aftermath of the collapse of Bear Stearns, Fannie Mae and Freddie Mac, and other big domestic and foreign financial institutions, Lehman Brothers collapsed, the press, politicians, and financial authorities started comparing the financial meltdown to 1929 and warning of the next Great Depression.

US companies got the message loud and clear that things looked very dicey (see Figure 1.1). The reaction was swift. They immediately began firing workers *en masse*. Month after month, on average, over the next 19 months, American firms put almost half a million workers on the street. By the end of this coordinated mass firing, 8.4 million US workers had joined the ranks of the unemployed. What synchronised this collective action was not a conspiracy of employers via a jointly reached decision, but a change in the state of animal spirits. The evidence is provided by the chart below, which shows that US business confidence fell through the floor in the immediate aftermath of the Lehman collapse. And as Figure 1.2 shows, British business confidence hit the skids starting around September 2007 when Northern Rock hit the rocks.[9]

Figure 1.1 United States Business Confidence

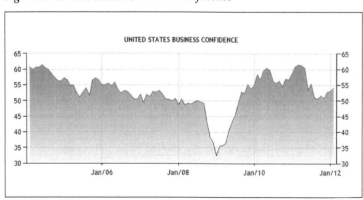

Source: www.tradingeconomics.com/Institute for Supply Management

Figure 1.2 United Kingdom Business Confidence

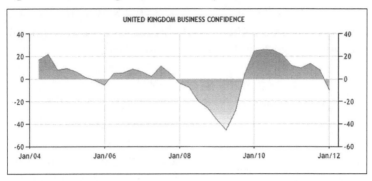

Source: www.tradingeconomics.com/ICAEW

The hysterical economy

The mass firings that occurred in the US, UK and other countries in the aftermath of the banking failures were coordinated by mass hysteria, not by any reasonably measured economic costs associated with banking-sector problems *per se*.

Take Lehman Brothers. Its collapse did not destroy or render less productive either its physical or human capital. The buildings Lehman owned and occupied on September 15, 2008, when it declared bankruptcy, were still there the next day. So were all of Lehman's Bloomberg terminals, computers and other equipment. Most important, in declaring bankruptcy, Lehman killed none of its bankers. They, together with all of their expertise, whatever its intrinsic value, sallied forth from Lehman's NY headquarters and other offices around the country and globe to seek new employment.

Yes, there was a direct economic loss. Not all the suddenly unemployed physical and human capital was re-employed or re-employed as productively. But most has found similar employment, although it has taken time for that to happen. But the total of such economic losses summed across Bear Stearns, Country Wide, Lehman

Brothers, Northern Rock, Royal Bank of Scotland, HBOS, BNP Paribas, UBS, Anglo-Irish Bank, MBIA, Citigroup, Merrill Lynch, Fannie Mae, Freddie Mac, Washington Mutual, Glitnir, Allied Irish, Bank of Ireland, Dexia, Landsbanki, AIG, Lloyds, Barclays, Bradford and Bingley, ING, ABN AMRO, Fortis and all other adversely impacted US and European commercial banks, investment banks, hedge funds, insurance companies, private equity funds, government sponsored agencies, credit unions and building societies, is trivial compared to the cost in lost output, jobs and human welfare arising from the general change in animal spirits associated with these financial failures.

The problem is the funeral, not the funeral arrangements

In reading the Vickers Report or, for that matter, the Dodd-Frank legislation in the US, one can easily come away with the impression that securing the payment system and keeping 'good' banks (retail/commercial banks dealing with households and small and medium-sized enterprises) from doing 'bad' things and investing in 'bad' ways, combined with quick resolution of insolvent banks – speedy financial funerals – is all that's needed to keep at least the 'good' part of the financial system safe.

But keeping the 'good part' of the financial system safe is not the central goal of financial reform. The central goal of financial reform is keeping the non-financial system safe – safe from crises in both the 'good' and 'bad' parts of the financial system.

If one considers what happened with the 28 institutions listed above that suffered major financial distress, one must conclude that however *ad hoc* and disorganised were the rescues and resolutions of these entities, the financial system was, in fact, kept safe. Even Lehman, to a considerable degree, lived for another day as major parts of its operations ended up being quickly acquired by Barclays and Nomura Holdings, Inc.

Treasuries, finance ministries and central banks in each of the affected countries stepped up to the plate and took bold and often drastic measures to ensure that (a) there would be no payments crisis and (b) that government capital would be substituted for private capital to offset runs by creditors, other than insured depositors, who were pulling their loans.

But despite the fact that the financial system was, in fact, kept safe, the economy was not kept safe from the financial system's trauma and near-death experience. To the public, in general, and business people, in particular, watching Bear Stearns collapse was no different to watching Lehman Brothers collapse. One was swiftly reorganised over the course of a weekend. The other was not. But both were venerable, venerated, and powerful financial institutions and the particulars of their 'resolution', i.e. the precise nature of their funeral arrangements, did not change the fact that both had died.

The funeral was the message, not the flowers. Most Americans weren't aware, nor cared, that Bear was 'resolved' by a pennies-on-the-dollar sale to J.P. Morgan while Lehman was 'resolved' by a pennies-on-the-dollar conveyance to its creditors. Yes, Lehman's resolution would be messier, take more time, but both had failed and both failures conveyed the same underlying message – the banks said 'trust me' and had shown they weren't to be trusted.

2. When Trust Takes a Holiday

Trust is another extremely precious and very fragile public good. Once it's there, more people can benefit from it without loss to its initial holders, and no one can be barred from trusting and being trusted. But once trust is lost, it can change individual economic behaviour and macro-economic outcomes instantly and dramatically.

Hitchhiking is a good example. When there were fewer cars, hitchhiking was commonplace. It wasn't a sign of indigence and almost everyone was willing to pick up riders because the chance that the hitchhiker would do one harm was very small. Over time, as society grew richer, only the poor needed to hitch a ride. But the poor, by definition, need money. And their ranks include pro-portionately more people with criminal records.

Hence, as the composition of hitchhikers changed, those that did hitchhike became more suspect and fewer were picked up. This, in turn, forced those with low incomes who could afford cars, but preferred to hitchhike, to buy their own wheels. The upshot was a further change in the perceived and actual distribution of hitchhikers, with an even higher percentage of hitchhikers being truly poor and, as a result, more suspect. Today, hitchhiking is a thing of the past because no one trusts hitchhikers. Nor, for that matter, do would-be hitchhikers trust those who might pick them up.

Another illustration of the precarious nature of equilibriums dependent on trust is the October 1982 Tylenol scare. Seven people in Chicago died over the course of a few days from ingesting Tylenol laced with cyanide. At the time, there were no safety-sealed containers. Everyone trusted that what was in Tylenol bottles was what it said on the label. When the Tylenol deaths were reported, there were 30 million unsealed bottles of the medication sitting on drug store counters around the globe. The number of tainted bottles implicated in the seven deaths was less than seven, since some relatives and friends of the initial deceased reached for the deceased's Tylenol to ease their own discomforts. They too then succumbed.

Virtually overnight, as news of the poison spread, all 30 million bottles became suspect. These bottles literally became a toxic asset and dropped like a rock in value, from $100 million to zero. Trust had taken a holiday.

Johnson & Johnson, the manufacturer, was forced to recall all 30 million bottles, throw them away, and distribute brand new Tylenol that could be trusted. How? By enclosing it in safety-sealed containers. This restored trust and the market was able once again to function.

Note that there are lots of toxic products for sale in drug stores. And Tylenol laced with cyanide might find a market among people who are trying to kill rodents in a benign manner. Thus, the problem was not selling Tylenol with cyanide. The problem was in selling Tylenol with cyanide as simply Tylenol, i.e. in not disclosing which Tylenol bottles had cyanide and which did not. Packaging cyanide in safety-sealed containers was, thus, an act of disclosure that overcame the inherent problem of trust involved in selling something that buyers couldn't verify they were receiving.

A third and more pertinent example of trust exiting stage left is the demise of complex, mortgage-backed securities that included liar loans, NINJA loans and no-doc loans. When word started to spread that some, if not many, if not most, of the mortgages underlying these securities had been fraudulently initiated, fraudulently rated, and fraudulently marketed, the bottom dropped out of this market as quickly as it dropped out of the Tylenol market in 1982. This, in turn, started raising suspicions of other products that banks and other financial institutions were marketing or holding.

Bear Stearns is a prime example. Before its collapse, Bear Stearns was the nation's seventh-largest financial company as measured by assets. It was also one of the oldest, having been founded in 1923. But the failure in 2007 of two of its subprime hedge funds brought the company's entire operation into question. Bear was leveraged 36 to 1, so all it took was a three per cent fall in the value of its assets to render the bank insolvent.

No one could say for sure what its assets were really worth or, for that matter, what debts it really owed. Its list of complex assets was enough to fill up a New York City phone book. It also had trillions in complex derivative positions, both long and short. Whether it was the US Treasury, the Securities and Exchange Commission, the US Federal Reserve, other regulatory bodies, or other major banks on the street – no one knew the true value of Bear because no one could look inside its bottles of assets and see if they had Tylenol or cyanide or both substances in particular ratios.

Amazingly, even the top traders within Bear were kept in the dark about its holdings. As a consequence, the valuation of the company depended, in very large part, on trust in the only parties that were privy and potentially knowledgeable. That was Bear's senior management. But stories had long circulated about Bear's CEO playing golf and bridge during business hours. These concerns about whether there was a responsible, trustworthy adult running the company coupled with the failure of the hedge funds led to a nine-month death spiral in which Bear's stock price fell from $172 per share in January 2007, to $93 per share in February 2008, to $57 per share in early March 2008, to just $2 per share in mid-March 2008.

Like any other bank, Bear borrowed short and lent long. What pushed Bear over the brink, forcing it to call for emergency help, i.e. from the Federal Reserve Bank of New York, was the collective decision by hedge funds to withdraw their uninsured brokerage account balances once rumour spread that other hedge funds were pulling out or might be pulling out.

Financial assets are valued for their expected return risk and liquidity. Brokerage accounts at Bear Stearns instantly acquired a lower expected return and a higher risk because, if everyone ran and the bank failed, the holders of these accounts would potentially be left, months if not years later, recovering pennies on the dollar. The same concern arose with respect to some of Bear's other liabilities. No one wanted to lend money overnight to Bear, let alone buy their medium- and long-term bonds. And Bear Stearns' bonds that were outstanding lost value both because they might not be paid off in full, but also because they could not readily be used as collateral for their holders' own borrowing. These bonds became less liquid because everyone presumed that others wouldn't readily buy them.

When Bear was 'resolved' by a Fed-organized sale to J.P. Morgan, the value of the firm had dropped below the appraised value of its New York headquarters building. But creditors were protected and Bear's resolution went, to a large extent, smoothly. Yes, the Treasury Secretary the Federal Reserve Chairman, and the New York Federal Reserve President, as well as their staff, had to spend some sleepless nights figuring out what to do. Yes, J.P. Morgan had to send in a team of bankers over the weekend of March 14th to determine what, if anything, they'd pay for Bear. And yes, the Federal Reserve had to close the deal by buying up $30 billion of Bear's particularly toxic assets. But not a single Bear creditor lost a penny.

In terms of the time and effort involved in resolving the nation's seventh largest bank, it's hard to conjure a smoother resolution. Yet the run on Bear did tremendous damage to the economy and the financial system. This bank's funeral, notwithstanding its still twitching corpse, put into doubt the contents of all the financial bottles full of opaque, if not inscrutable financial assets sitting on all the shelves of all the rest of the developed world's financial companies. And, over the ensuring year(s), one financial firm after another was subject to runs by non-insured creditors, requiring more bailouts, fire sales and nationalisations.

The run on Lehman differed in one important respect. The Treasury let Lehman fail for reasons that remain unclear. Perhaps Secretary Paulson wanted to test the market's reaction. If so, it was a costly experiment. It demonstrated to creditors that some sorts of resolutions could also wipe them out or generate very large losses.

The financial crisis' chief culprits: opacity, complexity and leverage

To summarise the argument made to this juncture, banks have leverage over taxpayers because they are caretakers of a public good, namely the financial market. When they go under, they take down financial intermediation with them. Their threat of failure and high average profitability gives them leverage over the public and politicians – in bad times, to extract bailouts, and in good times, to operate with minimal transparency and disclosure, to produce extremely complex products that can be sold at inflated prices to unsuspecting investors, and to take on extreme amounts of leverage.

Opacity, complexity and leverage are a very volatile mix when it comes to maintaining participation in a market place where participants can take their money and run. Trying to convince financial market participants that the system has been made safe, by assuring them they will quickly be able to collect their share of the pickings after they've been defrauded or misled, is not likely to carry the day.

Indeed, although the canonical explanation for demand deposits and other short-term credits is the sudden impatience to spend on the part of certain investors, the actual explanation appears to be the need, in a competitive environment, for banks to provide those investors who smell a rat the option to get out. Running on the bank at the first sniff of trouble is, then, what one would expect.

The spectre of large financial companies reneging or getting close to reneging *en masse* on financial promises raises three concerns in households' and business people's minds that has nothing to do with how 'smoothly' the reneging occurs. The first concern is that times are now bad or will collectively be viewed as bad because of the financial funerals, no matter the funeral arrangements. Second, having just been burnt or having just barely escaped being burnt, it will be hard to get people with funds readily to lend again. Third, if the financial sector promised X and delivered Y, which is much less than X, maybe the financial sector was lying about X and can't be trusted.

Traditional leveraged banking is unsafe at any speed

Although fraud played a major part in at least the US subprime crisis, fraud is not a necessary ingredient for financial collapse. The eurozone sovereign debt crisis is a case in point. With the exception of Greece, which fudged its fiscal books beyond the standard degree, no one has accused the other PIIGS – Portugal, Italy, Ireland, or Spain – of misrepresenting their ability to repay the loans they sold into the market.

But all the PIIGS securities have, nonetheless, caused a banking crisis because these 'safe' assets are being held, to a large degree, by eurozone banks. If these banks held none of this paper, there would be no crisis. The governments that issued these securities could default and stay on the euro with no fear of causing a eurozone financial system collapse.

There would also be no eurozone sovereign debt crisis had the eurozone banks not borrowed to buy these bonds. With no debt, the shareholders of the eurozone banks would have suffered larger capital losses and that would have been that. There would have been no fear of runs on eurozone banks, let alone the actual runs that have been taking place. But the eurozone banks are, in fact, highly leveraged and do, in fact, hold much of these troubled sovereign bonds.

Risk is easily misjudged. Indeed, financial experts seem as proficient at misjudging risk as judging it. Consider Figure 2.1 (p.72), taken from World Bank economist Mansoor Dailami's excellent study, 'Looking Beyond the Developed World's Sovereign Debt Crisis'.[10] In 2007, today's troubled eurozone-member country bonds were viewed virtually as safe as German bunds. Today, the spreads are enormous. And, as Figures 2.1-2.3 show (pp. 72-74), the downgrading of countries' sovereign bonds has produced a downgrading of the countries' banks, which disproportionately hold their own country's bonds.

Misjudging risk is, of late, not the exception, but the rule. In the months before they failed, both AIG and Lehman Brothers were rated AAA. And trillions of dollars in subprime collateralised Debt Obligations were rated AAA, when they should have been rated CCC. These examples highlight the fallacious presumption, which permeates Dodd-Frank, the Vickers Report, Basel I, II, and III, and banking regulation in general, namely, that assets can safely be judged to be safe.

17

3. The Vickers Report

Its self-limited charge

In its Executive Summary, the Vickers Commission takes as its goals a more stable and competitive banking system that will maintain Britain's position as a pre-eminent banking centre.

Stability is defined as 'greater resilience against future financial crises', 'removing risks from banks to the public finances', 'safeguarding retail deposits', 'operating secure payment systems', 'effectively channelling savings to productive investments' and 'managing risk'. And competition should be 'vigorous' and enforced by 'well-informed customers'.

The Commission views the Basel III and EU financial regulatory processes as heading in the right direction, but too lax in some dimensions. And, although the Commission suggests it is improving the regulatory setting, it concedes that, 'supervisory regulation will never be perfect' and that, in any case, it is 'not the role of the state to run banks'.

Hence, right off the bat the Commission admits defeat in achieving real financial stability. Furthermore, it takes the line that, as with any competitive industry, banks should live and die by the market. There is no discussion of banks as custodians of the financial market, of markets as public goods, or why banks need to be regulated in the first place.

Yet, just a few paragraphs further, we read that letting banks go bankrupt in 2008 was intolerable and that the financial system was on the point of seizing up when the government intervened. So there is an acknowledgment that banks are different, but it appears in the report only where it serves to support the Commission's conclusions.

The focus on keeping the banks from going bankrupt is telling. The Commission here and elsewhere suggests that the seizing up of the financial system – the point where lenders don't lend – occurs as a result of, and at the point of, bankruptcy, when, in fact, we've seen bank runs, i.e. the seizing up of financial markets, occur well short of formal bank failure. No major bank in the eurozone has gone bankrupt, but very many eurozone banks, both large and small, are currently having trouble borrowing from any entity except the European Central Bank, the European Financial Stability Facility, the IMF and the Federal Reserve.

The report assumes, without question, that banking, as we've known it, is essential, with the goal being to make it work better and accept the risk that it could take down the UK economy again and again. There is no discussion of what a fully safe banking system would look like or how it would compare with traditional banking. There is no acknowledgement that having banks fail, or effectively fail, but on a faster track and with more finesse, won't necessarily alter the impact of their failures on animal spirits and the economy's macro equilibrium.

To make the banks safer, if not safe, the report wants to enhance banks' abilities 'to absorb losses', 'make it easier and less costly to sort out banks that still get into trouble' and 'curb excessive risk taking'. The unstated presumption here is that losses will occur from taking risk, i.e. holding risky assets.

But there is no admission in referencing 'curbing excessive risk taking' that today's safe asset may well be tomorrow's risky asset. Yet the report acknowledges as much a few paragraphs later when it points out that restrictions on leverage as well as capital ratios (ratios of owners' equity to risk weighted assets) were inadequate because the risk weights didn't properly measure asset risk or its changes through time. Here, again, we have unpleasant facts surfacing in spots where they don't undermine the Commission's 'findings'.

Proposed reforms to enhance financial stability

The Commission indicates that if it had its druthers it would raise equity requirements across the board, internationally. But it fears putting the UK's financial system at a competitive disadvantage and, thus, tries to achieve financial stability through ringfencing retail banking operations and requiring that both ringfenced and non-ringfenced banks issue loss-absorbing debt.

Ringfencing retail banking entails having banks set up separate subsidiaries to handle retail customers, i.e. households and small and medium-sized business enterprises (SMEs). Since the Commission believes these customers are a captive audience and won't bank abroad, it feels free to apply its druthers to ringfenced banks and raise their equity requirements. Under Basel III all banks are to have equity equal to at least seven per cent of risk-weighted assets. The Commission would raise this capital requirement to 10 per cent in the case of ringfenced banks.

Ringfencing also entails restricting retail banks from engaging in certain types of 'bad' activities, such as proprietary trading, and in investing in certain types of 'bad' securities, such as derivatives. Ringfenced banks are intended, by the Commission, to withstand systemic financial crises; i.e. to permit core banking to continue in the UK for households and SMEs without government assistance in the case of financial meltdown. Ringfenced banks might, thus, be called bunker banks because they are meant to survive when the rest of the financial system blows up.

Ringfenced banks could and presumably would be owned by non-ringfenced banks, but the ringfenced banks would not invest in the non-ringfenced banks, although they would be able to borrow from such banks. This would help insulate ringfenced banks from suffering losses when non-ringfenced banks get into trouble.

The governance of ringfenced banks would also be organised to ensure their independence of sponsoring non-ringfenced banks, referenced by the Commission as 'banking groups'. Indeed, the chairman of the board as well as the majority of board members of ringfenced banks would be independent directors with no ties to the banking group to which the ringfenced bank belongs. The Commission estimates that ringfenced banks would hold roughly one sixth to one third of all UK bank assets. The remaining assets would be held by wholesale/investment banks catering, in large part, to global customers. In setting up this dichotomy between small/good/safe/tightly regulated retail banks with primarily British customers and big/bad/risky/less regulated wholesale banks with primarily foreign customers, the Commission is implicitly suggesting that government bailouts, in financial extremis, would be limited to the retail banks and that the bad, global banks would be left to sink or swim.

This suggestion is made with no recognition that foreign customers may be banking in the UK primarily because the British government stands ready to support its banks in times of financial crisis and that undermining that understanding may make investors much more likely to pull the plug (stop providing credits) the instant they get wind of problems with their banks.

Loss-absorbing debt refers to two things. The first is requiring banks to do more of their borrowing by issuing *contingent capital* – debt that converts to stock if certain bank distress markers are hit. Such markers would be short of full bankruptcy and, thus, provide banks with an automatic way of raising equity in times of crisis. The second is specifying that unsecured debt issued with a year or longer maturity, called *bail-in bonds*, automatically loses all claims to repayment in the event of bankruptcy.

The Commission recommends that both retail banks and banking groups have loss-absorbing capacity equal to between 17 and 20 per cent of total assets. Whether the requirement was 17 per cent or 20 per cent would be in the hands of regulators who would impose the 3 per cent higher requirement on banks that appeared less able to handle potential losses without recourse to taxpayer assistance. Large, systemically important banks, would also be subject to higher capital requirements to offset their 'too big to fail' implicit subsidy and to foster competition with smaller banks.

The Commission reports that prior to the crash, the UK leverage ratio (the ratio of all assets to owners' equity) was 40 to 1. Although the Commission asserts that Basel III's proposed 33 times leverage is too high, it recommends sticking with that limit except for large ringfenced retail banks for which it recommends up to a 25 times maximum leverage ratio depending on their size. The Commission places no additional restrictions on the leverage of wholesale investment banking groups.

The report properly takes umbrage at the government's being forced to bail out the banks. It views its reforms as limiting the chances that this will occur again. Indeed, it even suggests that it is 'eliminating the implicit government guarantee.'[11] And it calls for the Financial Services Compensation Scheme (FSCS), which insures retail deposits, to have first claim on any assets of failed banks that cannot cover their deposits.

Importantly, the report makes no recommendations about government oversight of security initiation. There is no government agency empowered to engage in the simplest elements of security verification, such as whether a mortgage applicant actually has the job, earnings, debts, assets and credit history she and the initiator allege or whether the house to be purchased is appropriately appraised.*

---

* Governments can do a better job than the private sector in such verification because it faces no conflict of interest in providing the information and because it has automatic access to tax, employment, and other government records that can be used in the verification process.

Nor does the report discuss the role of conflicts of interest facing rating companies; the failure of corporate governance on the part of bank boards of directors; the inability of creditors and shareholders, with diverse ownership rights, to monitor bank managers; the ability of top bank managers to expropriate shareholders; nor the failure of regulators to properly control the risk-taking behaviour of banks.

Many of these factors were of more concern in the US than in the UK financial collapse, but they are certainly of relevance. Yet, amazingly, the report proceeds as if these problems don't exist. On the contrary, throughout the report there are copious recommendations that simply presume proper risk rating and assessment, real corporate governance, and effective regulation.

Do the proposed reforms keep the 'good' banks safe?

One way to answer this question is to consider how a large UK ringfenced retail bank would fare under the Commission's policies were these policies currently in place and were the bank to invest exclusively in the safest securities around – UK gilts. These assets are rated AAA, so their risk weight is zero. Hence, the bank would meet the Commission's higher capital requirement. Indeed, it would meet any risk-weighted capital requirement since it holds no risky assets. The only restriction the bank would face on its investing and borrowing would come from the maximum leverage ratio, which would be set at 25.

Gilts are rated AAA and, thus, 'safe.' But are they really risk-free as a risk weight of zero suggests? No. The UK's debt to GDP ratio is currently 64 per cent. It is projected to reach 80 per cent over the next two years and could well continue to explode thereafter. Hence, the prospect for UK interest rates to rise and UK gilt prices to fall by at least four per cent is significant.[12] And that is all it would take to make the hypothetical bank insolvent.

Seven months ago, US Treasuries also enjoyed an AAA rating. But last August, Standard & Poors rated them AA+, notwithstanding the fact that the US debt to GDP ratio is only slightly higher than that of the UK. S&Ps concern was with the trajectory of US debt and with the inability of US politicians to agree on steps to achieve fiscal sustainability. Britain's political system seems to be able to make much quicker and more decisive policy changes as indicated by David Cameron's policies to date. But the UK economy is faltering, whereas the US economy is growing. Hence, UK debt may rise more rapidly over this decade than is true in the US.

The focus of Standard & Poor's and most other observers of fiscal conditions in the US, UK and other countries is on official debt. But economists have long known that what liabilities are classified as 'official' versus 'unofficial' is a matter of linguistics – how we label government receipts and payments.[13] In the post-war period, developed countries have accumulated massive liabilities to pay current and future retirees state pensions and healthcare benefits.

Including these and other implicit liabilities, measured in present value, with the official debt gives a picture of a country's true indebtedness. And if one nets out the projected taxes (also measured in present value) available to cover all these liabilities, one arrives at what economists call the present value *fiscal gap*.

The fiscal gap in the US is currently $211 trillion, based on projections made by the Congressional Budget Office. This is 14 times GDP and 12 per cent of the present value of GDP! The official debt, in contrast, is only $11 trillion. Hence, in the US, focus on the official debt is missing the forest for the trees. Moreover, the fiscal gap is growing at roughly $6 trillion per year since many of the unofficial liabilities represent, in effect, zero-coupon bonds that are coming due when the baby boomers retire. The closer the

US gets to having to make the principal payments on these bonds, the larger is their present value.

The story is much the same for the UK. As Figure 3.1 (p.75) shows, its fiscal gap is also enormous – almost 10 per cent of the present value of GDP. The chart was prepared by University of Freiburg economists, Bernd Raffelhüschen and Stefen Moog, based on projections made by the European Commission. What this figure means is that the UK must either raise taxes, immediately and permanently, to generate extra revenue in all future years equal, on an annual basis, to 10 per cent of GDP or cut non-interest spending, immediately and permanently, so that the annual spending cuts equal 10 per cent of GDP. A third option is to incur tax hikes and spending cuts that together amount to 10 per cent of each future year's GDP.

To put 10 per cent of GDP in perspective, the current ratio of UK revenues to GDP is about 35 per cent. Hence, closing its fiscal gap with taxes would require a roughly 30 per cent immediate and permanent hike in every tax levied in Britain.

Any country with a fiscal gap this large is in deep trouble. Yet the market views Italy as facing a much bigger fiscal problem than the UK even though its fiscal gap is only 2.4 times the present value of its GDP. Spain and Portugal are also in better fiscal shape than the UK when measured based on fiscal gaps. And Ireland is in slightly worse shape (see Figure 3.1, p.75). Were the market to start focusing on the UK's real indebtedness, it would, presumably, start discounting UK gilts as steeply as it's discounting the bonds of these four countries.

The point here is that the same 'risk managers', regulators, and rating companies that so badly misjudged the risks of subprime mortgages, real-estate investments, major financial institutions and sovereign debts may well be grossly under-assessing the true indebtedness of the UK and, thus, the true risk of UK gilts.

The primary risk associated with UK gilts is not default. The Bank of England is always available to print pounds to meet nominal repayment requirements. The primary risk is inflation. If, for example, the 'safe' bank being envisioned were borrowing short and investing long and inflation were to reach the roughly eight per cent value recorded in the early 1990s, long-term gilts would suffer huge price declines with much less change in the value of short-term gilts.

This would put our stylised 'safe' bank in the same position as so many US Savings and Loans in the late 1980s that failed after engaging in 'safe' banking – taking in short-term deposits and buying mortgages and real estate investments.

Are there prospects for inflation to increase, if not soar, in the UK in the short to medium term? You bet. The Bank of England's balance sheet has almost quadrupled since January 2007. And M4, the UK's standard measure of the money supply, has increased by 40 per cent. So far prices have risen by 14 per cent, but the relationship between the price level and the money supply has never been close on a short-term basis. Over long periods of time, the two series tend to move together. Hence, the conditions are in place for a very rapid inflation in the UK. As it is, the inflation rate is now running at 4.5 per cent per year – almost twice the 2.3 per cent rate recorded in 2007. And the UK is no stranger to much higher rates. In 1991, the inflation rate was 7.5 per cent. Moreover, UK debt has an average maturity of about 14 years, which is longer than that of most other developed countries.

Let's suppose, for argument's sake, that UK debt consisted entirely of 10-year bonds yielding the current 2.15 per cent rate. Now suppose inflation were to rise by four percentage points, equalling the inflation rate in 1991. By economic rights, the ten-year gilt yield would rise four percentage points to 6.15 per cent producing a 30 per cent decline in gilt prices. That's miles more than the four per cent asset price drop required to put our hypothetical ringfenced large retail bank out of business.

Yes, the Bank of England can take steps, if inflation takes off, to raise real interest rates and reduce the money supply. But raising real interest rates also raises nominal interest rates and, thus, will reduce the value of sovereign debt.

Moreover, if the British economy remains anaemic, the Bank may be very reluctant to take steps to limit inflation. The US Federal Reserve faced this dilemma in the early 1970s when the US economy was experiencing *stagflation*. It permitted inflation to get out of control until it was quelled, at an enormous cost, by Paul Volcker. When Paul Volcker tried to dampen inflation, US interest rates shot through the roof and stayed quite high for over a decade even as inflation fell dramatically.

Moreover, the temptation to monetise deficits is enormous for any government that is growing slowly, facing low inflation, and has authorized spending that is difficult to cut and levied taxes that are difficult to raise.

The US government used inflation during the 1970s to help finance the Vietnam War and, in the process, dramatically reduced the real value of outstanding Treasury bills and bonds. In the late 1990s, the Russian government used hyperinflation to help deal with an unsustainable fiscal policy. In its case, the hyperinflation, coupled with lagging indexation of nominal government pensions and military and civil service wage payments, permitted real cuts to government spending. And the examples go on. In the past century, 20 countries ran hyperinflations to deal with fiscal problems that were often less challenging than those facing the UK.

So, has the Commission proposed a banking structure that can keep safe even 'good' banks doing 'good' things, investing in 'safe' assets, meeting all criteria of 'prudent' regulators? The answer is no. The unfortunate economic fact of life is that there are no safe assets. Indeed, what the

Commission today views as the safest of assets, UK government bonds, appear to many observers (but not most, given prevailing yields), to be among the world's riskiest assets.

The Commission does not, of course, envision ringfenced retail banks investing solely in gilts. Yet there are banks today that are highly invested in 'riskless' sovereign bonds. Deutsche Bank is currently 'complying' with Basel III capital requirements while holding equity that represents only twp per cent of its assets; i.e. it is leveraged 50 to 1. The reason is that 85 per cent of its $3 trillion is invested in sovereign debt (including bonds of troubled eurozone member countries) and other 'riskless' assets. The ratio of its equity to the 15 per cent of its total assets that are deemed risky is 14 per cent, which is double Basel III's seven per cent floor.[14]

Figure 3.2 (p.76) shows, for different EU countries, holdings of domestic and foreign sovereign debt as a percentage of Tier 1 capital. Take Britain. Its banks hold domestic debt equal to 50 per cent of Tier 1 capital. But their overall sovereign debt holdings are three times their sovereign Tier 1 capital. Hence, a loss of one third in the value of these assets would wipe out the British banks. As just argued, such a loss is entirely conceivable for UK gilts and US Treasuries, let alone the other sovereign bond issues that British banks actually hold.

The Commission envisions ringfenced banks also investing mortgages, loans to SMEs, consumer loans, and corporate debt of various maturities. These would likely constitute the majority of such banks' assets. But the risk weights on these securities have in the past and could again be set at low levels. By overweighting 'safe' assets, banks, be they ringfenced or not, can effectively evade the Commission's capital requirements.

Before the subprime mortgage crisis hit, AAA-rated subprime mortgage securities received risk weights of just

20 per cent. This meant that a bank holding only such securities faced a capital requirement of just 1.6 per cent. This, in turn, means that a trivial loss in market value was all that was needed to bring such a 'safe' ringfenced bank down.

Do the proposed reforms keep the 'bad' banks safe?

No. If the good banks can invest in 'safe' assets, meet their capital and leverage requirements and end up going broke because what was safe turns out to have been risky, the 'bad' banks are not safe either since they are free to replicate the good banks' behaviour. But the bad banks have more leeway in their investments and also their liabilities, which, in some ways, make them safer than the good banks and, in other ways, make them riskier.

Bad banks are free to invest in more types of securities. Consequently, they have more ability to diversify than good banks. Finance 101 tells us not to put all our eggs in one basket – that when assets are risky and aren't dominated, you want to hold them all. This is clearly a case of the whole exceeding the sum of the parts.

Take the case of 100 assets that have the same expected return, the same variance, and aren't correlated. Now compare putting all your money in one of the assets versus spreading it out evenly over all 100. The risk of the former strategy is 100 times larger than the risk of the latter strategy – for the same expected return. Only if the 100 assets are perfectly correlated will the risk be as large as putting all your money in one basket. And if the assets are negatively correlated, not diversifying can be more than 100 times as risky as diversifying. Indeed, if the assets are sufficiently negatively correlated, one can produce a completely safe asset by investing in a portfolio of risky securities.

How could these ABCs of risk management have been overlooked by the Commissioners? The most plausible answer is they assumed there actually are completely safe securities in which retail banks can invest. This would explain, to some extent, keeping retail banks from holding particular types of investments. But, again, no truly safe assets exist. Cash, UK gilts, US Treasuries, German Bunds – none of these securities are safe in real terms. And there have been periods when these securities performed miserably compared to 'risky' equities. Given US and UK fiscal policies, gilts and Treasuries are, arguably, among the world's riskiest assets.

So setting store in absolute safety can't be the Commission's motivation. A different answer is that the Commissioners don't trust good bank bankers and good bank regulators to allocate and oversee bank asset portfolios in a manner that mitigates, rather than exacerbates risk. Bad banks, on the other hand, are being so trusted. They are free to invest in all manner of 'bad' assets, engage in 'bad' proprietary trading, hold 'bad' derivatives, and borrow from uninsured, 'bad' wholesale lenders and depositors who might pull their loans and deposits at a moment's notice.

True, bad banks are required to hold more capital, especially if they are large, and use contingent capital and bail-in bonds, in part, in their borrowing. But they can still operate with 33 to 1 leverage. Moreover, the bad bankers are free to try to pull the wool over the eyes of regulators when it comes to assessing the risk of the assets they purchase. Bankers are not bank owners, whose ownership of bank stock, particularly of large banks, is highly dispersed and whose control of 'their' banks is extremely weak. And because they aren't the owners, the bankers (i.e. bank management) have, for the most part, just one incentive in conducting their operations – 'make the money and run'.

How do bankers make more money? They take on more risk. More risky assets come with higher expected returns. Of course, such assets also come with larger downside risk. But bankers are paid base salaries and, so, are largely protected from downside risk. They also have the option to quit their jobs and find alternative employment. So it's primarily the upside risk that will determine their ultimate pay. Thus, the game becomes finding higher-yield, riskier assets that are sufficiently complex that regulators can't tell that they are riskier.

The Commissioners must have set their restrictions on investments in ringfenced retail banks in recognition of the fact that neither bankers nor regulators can be trusted to manage risk (to the extent risk is manageable) and that at least one part of the banking system should be kept safe from regulatory ineptitude or ignorance by giving regulators as simple a job as possible.

But in implicitly admitting that regulators can't regulate and that bankers can't be trusted, the Commissioners are also telling us that they expect bad banks, who are being permitted to do bad things, will not only do bad things, but also not get caught until it's too late, at which point the government will say: 'Sorry, you're on your own.'

But this experiment was tried with Lehman Brothers and failed miserably as 27 million currently unemployed and underemployed Americans can attest. It not only touched off a massive bank run that hit all financial institutions – characterised, not by lines of depositors desperately trying to withdraw their funds, but in the form of credit markets going into deep freeze, with no one lending to anyone except Uncle Sam. It also instantly destroyed business and consumer confidence, thereby coordinating a massive global recession.

But to give the Commission its due, it suggests, on page 32 of the report, that Lehman Brothers' failure would not likely have arisen had the Commission's proposed reforms been in place. According to the report:

> Lehman was heavily exposed to US sub-prime mortgages and over 30 times leveraged – a combination, which led creditors to stop providing funds as large losses began to materialise. When in late 2008 it ran out of liquid assets to sell to meet this withdrawal of funds, it filed for bankruptcy.

Richard Fuld's testimony to Congress on October 6, 2008 disputes this allegation, stating:[15]

> We did everything we could to protect the Firm, including: closing down our mortgage origination business; reducing our leveraged loan exposure; reducing our total assets by $188 billion, specifically reducing residential mortgage and commercial real-estate assets by 38 per cent; and dramatically reducing our net leverage so by the end of the third quarter in 2008 it was 10.5 times, one of the best leverage ratios on Wall Street at the time.
>
> Throughout 2008, the SEC and Fed actively conducted regular, and at times, daily oversight of both our business and balance sheet. Representatives from the SEC and the Fed were in our offices on a regular basis, monitoring our daily activities. They saw what we saw in real time as they reviewed our liquidity, funding, capital, risk management and mark-to-market process. Lehman Brothers had specific, dedicated teams that worked with the SEC and the Fed to take them through our finances and risk management, and answer any and all of their questions and provide them with all the information they requested. These were open conversations with seasoned and dedicated government officials.

In testimony to Congress April 20, 2010, Fuld stated:

> Speaking of asset valuations, the world still is being told that Lehman had a huge capital hole. It did not. The Examiner concluded that Lehman's valuations were reasonable, with a net immaterial variation of between $500 million and $2.0 billion. Using the Examiner's analysis, as of August 31, 2008 Lehman therefore had a remaining equity base of at least $26 billion. That conclusion is totally inconsistent with the capital hole arguments that were used by many to undermine Lehman's bid for support on that fateful weekend of September 12, 2008.

Let's assume that Fuld, as backed up by the Examiner overseeing Lehman's bankruptcy as well as the regulators supervising Lehman back in September 2008, is correct in asserting that Lehman had a leverage ratio of only 10.5 to 1. Let's also assume that Tier 1 capital, reported on September 11, 2008, was, indeed, 11.2 per cent of risk-weighted assets.[16] In this case, Lehman beat the Commission's leverage requirement by a factor of three and more than met its 9.5 per cent equity capital requirement laid out on page 120 of the report.

The report does call for additional *non-equity capital*, such as bonds that convert to stock if certain triggers are met, and *bail-in bonds* – longer term bonds that are subject to forfeiture in whole or in part if the triggers are flipped. This *loss-absorbing capacity* does not, however, necessarily activate until the bank has burned through its 9.5 per cent equity capital buffer and is being resolved by its regulator.

It should be noted, in this context, that Lehman had plenty of loss-absorbing capacity. In fact, all its liabilities were available to be lost. What the Commission is proposing is a means to ease and quicken the job of a regulator that resolves the collapse of a bad bank or the job of a bankruptcy judge that has to determine the division of assets among a bad bank's creditors in the context of insolvency.

The key point here, though, is that the Commission does not envision a bad bank that was in Lehman's situation, with, let us stipulate, a very low (by industry, not social standards) leverage ratio and a high capital ratio, experiencing a massive bank run that sets off or contributes to the spread of financial panic. Indeed, the report goes out of its way to suggest that with its proposals in place, Lehman's problems would not have arisen. Here's how the report says (on page 32) its policies would have helped in Lehman's case:

> Reforms to improve regulatory co-operation, the regulation of shadow banks and liquidity would have reduced the risks it posed. Greater use of central counterparties for derivatives would have limited contagion. If required in the US, bail-in and minimum loss-absorbency of 17%-20% of RWAs would have restricted the impact of losses and the consequential liquidity run. In the UK, the ring-fence would have insulated vital banking services of universal banks from contagion through their global banking and markets operations.

These four sentences are worth deconstructing. The first sentence is belied by the fact that the SEC and Federal Reserve were jointly and routinely examining Lehman's books in the nine months leading up to its collapse in mid-September 2008. Indeed, Fuld testified:

> Beginning in March of 2008, the SEC and the Fed conducted regular, at times daily, oversight of Lehman. SEC and Fed officials were physically present in our offices monitoring our daily activities. The SEC and the Fed saw what we saw, in real time, as they reviewed our liquidity, funding, capital, risk management and mark-to-market processes. The SEC and the Fed were privy to everything as it was happening. I am not aware that any data was ever withheld from them, or that either of them ever asked for any information that was not promptly provided.[17]

There have been no allegations that the SEC and the Fed were at loggerheads during this period of intense scrutiny of Lehman's books. Moreover, in the aftermath of Bear Stearns' demise, Treasury Secretary Hank Paulson was also focused intensely, as were top members of his staff, on Lehman's financial travails. Whether the government's regulatory bodies were co-operating in 2008 as well as they did, say, in 2006, is an open question. But there is no evidence that lack of regulatory cooperation was the cause of Lehman's failure.

The second sentence may or may not be true, but it doesn't answer the question posed, namely how the Commission's reforms would have prevented Lehman's collapse. The fourth sentence is also immaterial, since Lehman did not have a substantial retail client base.

The third sentence is conjecture predicated on supposition. The Commission supposes that, for example, the hedge funds that ran on Lehman to withdraw their uninsured funds in their brokerage accounts would have sat tight knowing that the company could not suffer a loss on the value of its assets in excess of 20 per cent. And it supposes that Lehman's other short-term lenders would have made the same assumption – this at a time when Lehman's stock price was vaporising.

The fact is that Lehman's solvency was predicated on trust, particularly the trust that the company was still trusted. As soon as that premise was questioned by the market, as revealed by Lehman's stock price, the run was on. The knowledge that some creditors would get burnt quickly and thoroughly would not have assuaged other creditors from rushing to get their money out. In point of fact, Lehman creditors ended up with only 20 cents on the dollar, not the 80 cents on the dollar the Commission presumes would be available for residual creditors who were not automatically wiped out.[18]

To be fair to the Commission, it's actually not 80 cents on the dollar, but 100 cents on the dollar being assumed since residual creditors wouldn't have to share the remaining assets with wiped-out creditors. And the 20 cents on the dollar needs, correspondingly, to be changed to 25 cents on the dollar. But 25 cents on the dollar, pound, euro, etc. is a long way from 100 cents, which is what *bail-out* creditors can retrieve if they run fast enough.

The creditors that appeared to have run first from Lehman were its roughly 100 hedge fund clients who were using Lehman as their prime broker. They had cash in brokerage accounts along with financial assets of varying degrees of liquidity that had been purchased on margin, i.e. with money borrowed from Lehman. The assets so purchased were often pledged by Lehman as collateral for its own borrowing via the process known as *re-hypothecation*. Consequently, the hedge funds knew that if Lehman got into trouble and was unable to repay its debts, the hedge funds' assets might be retained by Lehman's other creditors, meaning the hedge funds would lose those assets.

This gave the hedge funds a huge incentive to try to cash out their positions before other hedge funds and other creditors pulled out of Lehman. And while Lehman's glossy report on September 11, 2008 showed it had significant (for the industry) equity on its books and relatively low leverage, everyone knew that this equity cushion was miles too small to matter and the leverage was miles too high to help save the day if everyone panicked at once.

According to Fortune Magazine:

> Some hedge funds that used Lehman's London office as their 'prime broker' had their assets frozen, setting off a run on prime brokers Goldman Sachs and Morgan Stanley as US hedge funds pulled out their assets to avoid getting frozen if either firm failed. Goldman and Morgan were close to running out of cash when the government saved them by making them bank companies with access to the Fed's lending facilities. Bailout! Bailout! GE Capital was having trouble rolling over its borrowings, and was rescued by a government guarantee program. Bailout! Then there was American International Group, the now infamous AIG, which required a 12-figure rescue.
>
> Had Goldman, Morgan Stanley, GE Capital, AIG, and several giant European banks not gotten bailouts and instead failed, even capital-rich J.P. Morgan Chase would have gone under, because it wouldn't have been able to collect what these and other players owed it. There would have been trillions in losses, worldwide panic, missed payrolls, and quite likely the onset of Great Depression II. That's why we needed a bailout. And why we got it.[19]

The UK has no limit on re-hypothecation of clients' assets. But this practice of taking a customer's property and putting it at additional risk is completely ignored by the report; the term 're-hypothecation' appears not once. Nor does the term 'counter-party risk'. Yet it is the enormous volume of this counterparty banking activity that helped call into question whether banks' book values of equity were for real or were simply laughing stocks.

Nonetheless, the Commission blithely assumes that (a) smoother resolution/bankruptcy procedures (via contingent capital and bail-in bonds) will keep nervous bail-out creditors – creditors with no precise knowledge of the degree to which a bank's books can be trusted – from panicking if they see or suspect that others are panicking and (b) that the UK government will stand back and watch bad banks freeze up and fail because their clients are primarily 'financially sophisticated' large companies and in large part foreigners.

Again, this experiment was run in the US and within days of Lehman being allowed to fold the Federal Reserve was forced to buy up over $14 trillion in financial sector assets – almost one year's GDP – to keep, as the Fortune quote affirms, every major US financial firm from going belly up.

The Commission also seems to ignore the fact that the UK is securing international business and has the world's largest financial system, measured relative to GDP, precisely because its treasury and central bank are standing by to provide 'lender of last resort', 'insurer of last resort', and 'dealer of last resort' services.* Taking away those guarantees as the report strongly intimates it advocates, but can't quite spit out in clear prose, has the potential to make creditor runs more, not less, likely and more, not less, rapid notwithstanding the report's proposed additional capital and loss-absorbency capacity.

Richard Fuld, like so many big bankers, gambled excessively with his bank and the country paid the price. But when Fuld says that what happened was not a failure to play by the rules, but the outcome of collective panic, he's right. Let's listen.

---

* 'Insurer of last resort' refers to the treasury and central bank of a country bailing out insurance companies in a financial crisis as well as potentially standing behind credit default swaps and other market-based insurance products whose counterparties may not be able to cover their positions. Perry Mehrling coined 'dealer of last resort' in his excellent book, *The New Lombard Street – How the Fed Became the Dealer of Last Resort,* Princeton University Press, 2011. 'Dealer of last resort' refers to central banks standing ready to buy and sell private-sector securities, such as securitized mortgages during financial crises traders/brokers panic and take to the hills.

... ultimately what happened to Lehman Brothers was caused by a lack of confidence. This was not a lack of confidence in just Lehman Brothers, but part of what has been called a storm of fear enveloping the entire investment banking field and our financial institutions generally. As evidenced by Congress' efforts to pass an emergency rescue plan, there is a systemic lack of confidence in the system that without emergency intervention could result in an across the board failure. While all investment banks were prepared for shocks in the market, none of us was prepared for this one. And all of us are now forever changed. Investment banks depend on the confidence and trust of employees, clients, investors and counterparties.

Has the commission made UK banking safe?

To summarise, the Commission's proposed reforms make neither good banks nor bad banks safe. Banks are supposed to be custodians of financial markets. Instead, they are gambling with this public good. They borrow to the hilt. They make promises they can't keep. They back their promises with assets they won't disclose. They pay rating companies to bless their mistakes. They bribe politicians to look the other way. They run rings around regulators. They make sure shareholders and creditors have little say. And they buy off their most risk averse and best-informed creditors by telling them they can take their money out before everyone else provided they get there quickly.

The Commission addresses none of these problems. Instead it focuses on fixing a problem that didn't arise in the financial crisis, namely a breakdown in the payment system and the loss of deposits of households and small and medium size business. It also limits proprietary trading and the use of derivatives, neither of which was the direct cause of any of the major bank failures.

Worst of all, the report ignores the inherent instability of leveraged, 'trust-me banking', notwithstanding what just happened, namely a financial earthquake brought about, in large part, by the disclosure of mortgage securitisations and real-estate purchases of unknown toxicity (shades of the Tylenol scare), followed by a snowballing loss of trust in banks and bankers, followed by a loss of trust in other people's trust of banks and bankers, followed by wholesale panic and a run to retrieve one's money.

Given this, the only conclusion one can reach is that the Commissioners, realising they couldn't make conventional banking, and, thus, the economy, safe and being unwilling to confront the City, with its political protectors, needed to follow the lead of Dodd-Frank and invent banking problems whose 'cures' would not unduly perturb traditional banking. The result is a thick, highly repetitive report, which undercuts most of it conclusions with major caveats, offers antidotes to most of its prescriptions, and appears to maximise regulatory cost per pound of benefit. Most troubling is the report's failure to give clear guidance on questions like the proper triggers at which contingent capital is to absorb losses, how to calculate the degree of bail in required of bail-in bonds, and the feasibility of establishing, within large banking groups, ringfenced retail bank subsidiaries who will be owned, but not controlled by the banking groups.

I'll return to these concerns later, but for now, I want to lay out a safe banking system, namely Limited Purpose Banking, and consider the Commission's analysis of it.

4. A Safe and Practical Alternative: Limited Purpose Banking

Suppose we could rewind the clock and ask the Commissioners to start from scratch in reviewing and reshaping the financial system with their first task being to clarify the proper role, goals and structure of the financial system so as to guide financial reform.

What would these desiderata be?

Each Commissioner would likely have had a different list, but had it polled the public, it would likely have ended up with the following consensus:

The proper role, goals and structure of the financial system

1. The financial system's role is intermediation, not gambling.

2. The financial system should be transparent and provide full disclosure.

3. The financial system should never collapse or put the economy at risk.

4. The financial system should not require government guarantees and threaten taxpayers.

5. The financial system should be sufficiently well structured as to require limited regulation.

6. The financial system's intermediation practices should enhance economic performance.

This list differs in critical ways from what the Commission set out to do, which was to 'create a more stable and competitive basis for UK banking in the longer term', achieve 'greater resilience against future financial crises', and produce a banking system that is effective and efficient in 'removing risks from banks to the public finances', 'safeguarding retail deposits, operating secure payment systems, channelling savings to productive investments, and managing financial risks'.[20]

In particular, the Commission accepted that the financial system will suffer from future crises, that it will continue to take risks, that it will be left with primary responsibility for managing its 'own' risks, notwithstanding its risks to other banks and the economy, and that it will work to remove, but not actually eliminate, risks to the public finances. Thus, the Commission began its critical mission by declaring defeat with as much face as could be saved.

The Commission's presumption that the financial system can 'manage risk' is particularly troubling. If the financial crisis has taught us anything, it's that banks are in the business of making, not managing risk. Indeed, their 'risk management' coupled with the inherent instability of opaque, trust-me banking, has done grave and lasting damage to millions upon millions of people around the planet.

Conceptually, financial intermediaries can help us pool idiosyncratic risks, and they can help us allocate aggregate risks (what economists call aggregate shocks) to those best able to absorb them. But they can't bear risk. Banks, insurance companies, hedge funds, private equity funds, building societies and their ilk are corporations. Corporations aren't people. They don't laugh, sing, love, hate or cry, and they don't bear risk.

Only people can bear risk. The current owners of financial corporations, their stockholders and their contingent owners, i.e. their creditors, are the first-line shock absorbers when financial corporations get into trouble. But as we've seen, taxpayers, workers, retirees and even children can end up getting very badly hurt when we let banks and other financial market makers operate under the existing rules of the game.

In opting for financial business as usual, albeit with some new window dressing, the Commission maintained the pretence that banks can vanquish risk. They can't. And, in pretending they can, banks make things riskier. The Great Crash of 2008 and its global economic fallout reflects man-made risk – risk manufactured by a financial system that ran a massive confidence game that, when uncovered, failed catastrophically.

Once one realises that banks, as structured, are risk makers, not risk managers, the immediate question is how to limit their actions to their legitimate purpose, namely financial intermediation. The answer, Limited Purpose Banking, is remarkably simple. Indeed it can be summarised in just eight points.

Limited Purpose Banking's simple design

1. All financial companies protected by limited liability can market just one thing – mutual funds.*

2. Mutual funds are not allowed to borrow, explicitly or implicitly, and, thus, can never fail.

3. Cash mutual funds, which are permitted to hold only cash, are used for the payment system.

4. Cash mutual funds are the only mutual funds backed to the buck.

5. Tontine-type mutual funds are used to allocate idiosyncratic risk.

6. Parimutuel mutual funds are used to allocate aggregate risk via direct or derivate betting.

---

* Open-end mutual funds are known as unit trusts in the UK. They invest in liquid securities and the shares (units) held by owners of the unit trusts can be redeemed with the trust managers. But the mutual funds that would arise under Limited Purpose Banking would be closed-end as well as open-end. Closed-end mutual funds buy and hold financial securities or real assets and have no obligation to buy back shares on demand.

7. The Financial Services Authority (FSA) hires private companies working only for it to verify, appraise, rate, custody and disclose, in real time, all securities held by mutual funds.

8. Mutual funds buy and sell FSA-processed and disclosed securities at auction. This ensures that issuers of securities, be they households or firms, receive the highest price for their paper.

Drawing the right line in the sand

The historic Glass-Steagall legislation, which the Dodd-Frank bill and the Vickers Report built upon, drew a line between commercial banks and investment banks. The notion is that commercial banks (ringfenced retail banks) are good banks, which will be kept good by limiting the nature of their customers, the type of their investments and the durability of their creditors, and by bailing them out if need be.

Investment banks will be bad banks, which can have bad customers (big firms and foreigners), invest in bad things, like derivatives, have bad creditors, and be left high and dry if they get into trouble. As argued above, this experiment failed spectacularly when Lehman was permitted to fail. Not only did US banking policy shift instantly to preventing any more large bank or insurance company failures, the US government also permitted the remaining big investment banks to jump back over the line by simply changing their names from investment to commercial banks.

The fact that Goldman Sachs and Morgan Stanley could switch from being investment banks to being commercial banks from one day to the next, with no discernible change in behaviour, shows that the Glass-Steagall, Dodd-Frank, and Vickers Commission line is based on form, not function. In repeating the canard – that we can make banks good by calling them good – the Commission failed to admit an essential fact, namely that all financial companies, regardless of their titles, are engaged in the same business, namely opaque, leveraged financial intermediation.

Even an everyday life insurance company is engaged in making promises it secretly knows it can't keep. These companies sell mortality (life) insurance to young people and longevity (annuity) insurance to old people. In both cases they promise to pay their policyholders when their loss occurs. Their leverage arises in the form of taking in money, which they call 'premiums', but which could just as well be called 'borrowings', and promising to pay back money when their client dies, in the case of mortality insurance, or lives, in the case of longevity insurance. But like financial intermediaries that call themselves 'banks', life insurance companies also make promises they can't keep and, consequently, can fail.

In selling mortality insurance, these companies promise to pay out to decedents regardless of whether or not their mortality assumptions are right or wrong. To see this, suppose swine flu were to return and wipe out over 2.5 per cent of the population as it did starting in the great worldwide pandemic that began in 1918, what would happen? The answer is simple. Every life insurance company in the world would go under. None of these companies have sufficient reserves to cover such a high death rate, just as no bank has sufficient reserves to cover a significant run.

Collectively, in the US, life insurance companies have roughly $20 trillion of life insurance in force, but only a few billion dollars tucked away in state insurance reserves. These companies assert they are 'managing their risk' by marketing longevity policies as well as mortality policies so that when they lose on the one, they gain on the other. But this ignores the fact that swine flu differentially kills young adults, who are differentially life insurance policyholders, and is much less effective in killing the elderly. It also ignores the fact that swine flu could break out concurrent with the discovery of a breakthrough cure for cancer.

In that state of the world, the 'safe' hedge put on by selling both types of policies becomes an LTCM portfolio. LTCM refers to Long Term Capital Management – an enormous, 250 to 1 leveraged hedge fund that collapsed spectacularly in 1998 when its 'perfect' hedges turned out to be perfectly correlated in the 'no-way-this-can-happen' state of the world that chose to prevail.

The US life insurance industry also writes whole-life and related cash-surrender polices that are no different, really, from checking accounts. The policyholder pays in (lends the insurance company) more money than is needed to buy the life insurance packaged in her whole-life policy, and the insurance company promises to return the extra funds, with interest, whenever the policyholder elects to cash out her policy.

During the financial crash of 2008, the life insurance industry had roughly $3 trillion in outstanding cash surrender policies. Had AIG been allowed to fail, the holders of these cash surrender policies would have cashed in their policies forthwith; i.e. we would have observed a run on the life insurance companies to complement the runs on the banks and money market funds. In fact, the decision by the Treasury and Fed to bail out AIG may have been motivated, in large part, by a concern about a run on these unnamed demand deposits.

Limited Purpose Banking's line in the sand

Limited Purpose Banking (LPB) draws its line in the sand not between commercial and investment banks or between banks and non-banks, but between financial intermediaries with and without limited liability. All banks, insurance carriers, hedge funds, and other financial intermediaries with limited liability would be LPB banks, and all LPB banks would operate strictly as unleveraged mutual fund (unit trust) holding companies; i.e. they would not be permitted to borrow, including going short, to invest in risky assets. Their only permitted function would be to market 100 per cent equity-financed mutual funds.

To ensure LPB banks operate on a completely risk-free basis, their investment banking activities would be run strictly as consulting services and leave the banks with no skin in the game. And all brokerage activities would be done via matching of buyers and sellers of securities, with no exposure of any kind at any time.

Note that the mutual funds marketed by mutual fund holding LPB companies, are, themselves, small banks with 100 per cent capital requirements in all situations – what economists call *states of nature*. Hence, under LPB neither the mutual funds themselves, nor their holding companies, the LPB banks, could ever go bankrupt. Unlike Simon Johnson's call for breaking up large banks, LPB permits large banks to morph into large mutual fund holding companies that operate large numbers of completely safe (in the sense that they themselves can't fail) small banks, namely mutual funds. These mutual funds would be both open and closed-end, with in-kind redemption rules governing open-end funds to preclude any question of payout in the case of significant simultaneous redemptions.

The role of financial regulation

Because every financial corporation would be a mutual fund holding company marketing non-leveraged mutual funds that could never go broke, financial collapse would be a thing of the past. So would non-disclosure, insider-rating and the production of fraudulent securities. A single regulatory body – such as the Financial Services Authority – would establish, as the National Institute for Clinical Excellence does for medicine, what is and isn't known about various securities.

Every security bought or sold by the mutual funds

would be processed by the FSA. The FSA would hire companies that work exclusively for it to verify and disclose in real time all details of all securities being bought, sold or held by the mutual funds.[21] For example, in the case of a mortgage, it would verify the employment status, current and past earnings, credit history and credit rating of the mortgage applicant. The companies working for the FSA would also appraise the value of the house the applicant seeks to purchase. Most importantly, it would disclose all details about the security on the web at the time it is issued and on an on-going basis over its maturity.

Issuers of the security would be free to post their own assessments of the paper they are issuing, including private ratings that they have purchased. But the public would no longer need to trust people and institutions that have proven they aren't trustworthy.

The LPB auction market

Once a new security is initiated by an LPB bank, processed by the FSA and fully disclosed on the web, it would be put up for auction to the mutual funds being run by the LPB banks. This would ensure that issuers of bonds and stock receive the highest prices (pay the lowest interest rates) for their securities.

The FSA's role may sound like lots of state intervention in the financial marketplace. It's actually the opposite. The remit of the FSA would be very narrow. Finally, most of its job would be done by the private sector – by private, non-conflicted, third-party appraisers, and risk-raters hired by the government.

The FSA will not ban any securities. It will disclose them. By analogy, the FSA will ensure that a bottle with cyanide is labelled cyanide, not Tylenol, so that people who shop in financial stores (mutual funds) will know what they are buying.

We know from long experience that markets don't work

without well-enforced rules of law. The FSA sets financial rules of law, namely, that you can't sell what you don't have. But it doesn't say what financial products can or can't be sold.

The market will no longer be forced to rely on 'trustworthy' bankers to honestly initiate securities, whether they be mortgages, consumer loans, small-business loans, large corporate debt issues or equity offered by small or large businesses.

Wouldn't LPB restrict credit?

No. Under LPB, people who seek to lend money to home buyers would simply purchase shares in a mutual fund investing in mortgages, with the money going directly to the mutual fund (not to the bank sponsoring the fund) and from there to the home buyer in return for his or her mortgage. Those wanting to lend to small (large) companies would buy mutual funds investing in small firm (large firm) commercial paper. Those wishing to finance credit card balances would buy mutual funds investing in those assets.

Credit is ultimately supplied by people, not via some magical financial machine. And every dollar people want to lend would be provided to borrowers via mutual funds or in direct person-to-person loans or via non-LPB banks that are not protected by limited liability.

Limited Purpose Banking is extremely safe compared to our extremely risky and, indeed, radical status quo. Indeed, it's hard to think of LPB as being anything but highly conservative in terms of maintaining the safety of the financial system, requiring disclosure to preclude fraud in financial markets, and keeping bankers from imposing unaffordable costs on taxpayers.

Furthermore, LPB is, in large part, already in place, at least in the US. The US mutual fund industry has some 10,000 individual mutual funds that collectively hold about

30 per cent of US financial assets. The number of mutual funds actually exceeds the number of banks, and most Americans do most of their banking through mutual funds since mutual funds are the principal repositories of their 401(k), IRA and other tax-favoured retirement accounts. A sizeable share of these 10,000 mutual funds is involved in credit provision. And roughly half of mutual fund assets are credit instruments.[22]

Another example of the use of mutual funds to provide credit, specifically mortgages, is the covered-bond markets of Denmark, Sweden and Germany. The covered bonds are offered by banks through what looks, to a very large degree, like mutual funds. Indeed, if the banks selling covered bonds were precluded from insuring bondholders against default risk, the covered bond markets in Europe would simply constitute LPB mortgage mutual funds.

Moreover, large borrowers have been voluntarily bypassing the banks over the last quarter-century, and borrowing most of what they need from the capital markets. In other words, they are already getting most of the credit they need from the kinds of mutual fund that LPB would create.

Using cash mutual funds for the payment system

Under LPB, cash mutual funds would be used for the payment system. Cash mutual funds hold only cash (physical currency), pay no interest, and never break the buck. They are the only mutual funds that don't break the buck, for the simple reason that, apart from the fees charged for holding investors' cash, there is always one pound in the vault for every pound invested. The prospectus of every other mutual fund would state in big letters at the top – 'This Fund Is Risky and Can Break the Buck.'

If a Reserve Primary Fund (the huge money market fund that went under in 2008) wants to purchase 'safe' securities, like AAA-rated Lehman Brothers bonds, that fact will be disclosed in broad daylight on the web. So no one can claim they didn't know what was being done with their money. Such money market funds would be marked to market on a continual basis, and the mutual fund holding company sponsoring the mutual fund would be precluded from using any of its assets to support the buck of any mutual fund. Hence, from day one of the introduction of LPB, some money market mutual funds will break the buck and the public will get used to that happening.

Holders of cash mutual funds would access their cash at ATMs, via writing cheques or by using debit cards. Thus, cash funds represent the checking accounts of the new financial system and are used for the payment system. This is the 'Narrow Banking' component of Limited Purpose Banking. But as is clear, LPB goes far beyond Narrow Banking, not just in making the payment system perfectly safe, but in making the entire financial system perfectly safe.

Idiosyncratic insurance mutual funds

The mutual funds that insurers would issue would differ from conventional mutual funds. First, purchasers of such insurance mutual funds would collect payment contingent on either personal outcomes or economy wide conditions or, potentially, both.

This lets people buying an insurance mutual fund share risk with one another. Second, they would be closed end mutual funds, with no new issues (claims to the fund) to be sold once the fund had launched.

Take, for example, a three-month, closed-end, life insurance fund sold to healthy males aged 50 to 60. Purchasers of this fund would buy their shares on, say, January 1, 2011, and all the monies received would be invested in three-month Treasury bills. On April 1, 2011 the pot, less the fee paid to the mutual fund, would be divided among those who had died (their estates) over the three months in proportion to how much they contributed.

Hence, Limited Purpose Banking permits people to buy as much insurance coverage as they'd like. The most important feature, though, is that these insurance mutual funds pay off based not just on diversifiable risk, but also based on aggregate risk. That is, if more people die than expected, less is paid out per decedent.*

For students of financial history, this is simply a *tontine*, a financial security that dates to 1653. Tontines were an everyday financial institution for over two centuries. The French and British governments raised money by issuing tontines. The New York Stock Exchange first met under the buttonwood tree, but its members quickly moved into a drier, warmer space, named the Tontine Coffee House.

Tontines were paid off to shareholders if they lived, not if they died. But the payoff can be predicated on death or any other idiosyncratic risk, including property losses, disability, medical costs, accidents, etc.†

In all cases, the fund's pot is given and is paid out to the 'winners' (those suffering a loss). Since these are fully collateralised bets, there is no liability visited upon unsuspecting taxpayers. The pot of this and all other LPB mutual funds constitute natural financial firewalls – something that is desperately needed and entirely missing from our current financial system.

To repeat, if and when a virulent form of Swine Flu really hits, our current financial system is set up to ensure not just widespread human death, but also widespread

---

* As discussed in *Jimmy Stewart is Dead* (Kotlikoff, 2010), life insurance mutual funds could also combine bets on whether or not survivors experience documented changes in their health status that would make them ineligible for buying into life insurance mutual funds restricted to those in good health. I.e. this would be insurance pools against becoming uninsurable.

† In the case of property, auto insurance, other casualty insurance, and health insurance, one's claim would be proportional to one's loss as well as one's contribution to the fund.

financial death. LPB is set up to ensure the financial system is unaffected.

Parimutuel insurance mutual funds

The final point is that insurance mutual funds can be set up to bet exclusively on aggregate outcomes, like a particular company going bankrupt or the nation's mortality rate exceeding a given level. Shareholders in such closed-end funds would specify whether they were betting on the event occurring or not. If the event occurs, those betting on the occurrence take the pot (the holdings of the mutual fund less the fee charge by the mutual fund managers) in proportion to their shares. If the event doesn't occur, those betting against the occurrence take the pot based on their shares.

If bets like this on non-personal outcomes sound familiar, there's a reason. This is simply pari mutuel betting, which has been safely used at racetracks around the world since 1867. There is no recorded instance in which a bet on a horse at any racetrack ever cost taxpayers a single penny.

Let's consider some examples of LPB parimutuel funds. Suppose the elderly want to bet with the young on whether mortality exceeds a given rate. The elderly would bet on low mortality, because if mortality is low their longevity (annuity) tontines would pay less. The young would bet on high mortality, because if mortality is high, their life insurance tontines would pay less. So each side hedges the other. This is allocating aggregate risk, which a proper financial system needs to do. It is not insuring against aggregate risk, which no financial system can do.

What about modern financial instruments like CDS and options? Do they disappear? Not at all. LPB combines modern and ancient finance. A closed-end parimutuel fund that entertains bets on a company's stock exceeding a given price on a fixed date is just an option. A credit default swap

(CDS) is a parimutuel fund that stages bets on a company's defaulting on its bonds over a fixed period of time. A collateralised debt obligation (CDO) is a mutual fund that invests in particular types of loans and pays out the pot to shareholders based on pre-specified sharing rules. These clear sharing rules allow the different parties to take more or less leverage *vis-à-vis* each other, but they preclude leveraging the taxpayer.

LPB can thus provide the economy with as much legitimate leveraging as the population desires. This leveraging can, as just indicated, occur within mutual funds, or by mutual funds buying up the mortgages, notes, bonds and other debts of households, small and medium-sized proprietorships and partnerships and corporations.

Note that these 'bad' derivative securities that the Vickers Commission precludes the ringfenced retail banks from holding are important forms of risk sharing. What's truly bad about these securities is not their intrinsic nature, but rather their issuance by leveraged banks and insurance companies who aren't always able to pay off what they owe. In contrast, under LPB, insurance mutual funds always involve fully collateralised bets, i.e. all the money in play is on the table, not in some banker's imagination or in the pockets of taxpayers who need to bail out an AIG after selling nuclear economic war insurance in the form of unbacked CDSs.

Democratising and modernising finance

LPB takes control of finance away from large, secretive, unaccountable banks, insurance companies and other financial corporations and puts it in the hands of individuals via their mutual fund investments. Individuals who are very risk averse will buy shares of mutual funds that invest in shorter-term, safer assets. Individuals who are less risk averse will invest in mutual funds that hold riskier assets. Unlike the current system, the public will have a much better understanding of the risks they are accepting. And, most importantly, the public will no longer be exposed to the risk of losing their jobs and their lifetime savings through man-made financial system collapse.

Implementing LPB would be much more difficult without the internet, which would be used, not only as it is today, to manage mutual fund investments, holdings, and withdrawals, but also to disclose, in real time, mutual fund securities and to run the mutual fund securities auctions.

To some, the idea that traditional banking would disappear seems incredible. But the history of human progress is one incredible story after another. Traditional farming, traditional retailing, traditional horse and buggy transportation, traditional media, traditional everything has and will change.

The main reason we are still inflicted with a millennium-old financial system that has failed repeatedly through the ages is that traditional banking is being implicitly subsidised by governments, or rather politicians who are willing to bail out the banks when they get into trouble. This financial guarantee is not simply motivated by public interest. The financial sector is well adept at influencing the politicians through campaign donations and promises of very high-paying jobs once they leave office.

The introduction of parimutuel funds could bring forth much of the financial innovation that Robert Shiller and others have been so passionately advocating.[23] We should, for example, be able to bet with people from other countries that our economy will do poorly and theirs will do well. This will hedge us against the risk of recession. Such risk sharing would, under LPB, be run through a parimutuel fund where the bet is on US GDP growing, say, more or less than 3.5 per cent.

In general, there is nothing in Limited Purpose Banking that limits legitimate financial innovation. But illegitimate, highly leveraged, financial 'innovation', involving the sale of undisclosed snake oil, will, as it should, find few or no takers.

Assuaging concerns about Limited Purpose Banking

LPB doesn't limit borrowing by firms or households. Indeed, thanks to the FSA's services and the auction mechanism, it should enhance their ability to borrow as well as sell equity. This is particularly true of small and medium-sized enterprises.

LPB eliminates leverage by financial intermediaries, where leverage entails great macroeconomic risk. Modigliani-Miller tells us that leverage doesn't matter unless there are bankruptcy or information costs, in which case equity is preferred. In banking, bankruptcy costs are arguably as high as it gets, and the FSA is designed to dramatically reduce information costs.

In eliminating bank leverage, LPB eliminates the leverage intermediaries have over taxpayers during a financial crisis in credibly threatening financial meltdown if they aren't bailed out. Eliminating fractional reserve banking will make the money multiplier 1, but it won't reduce the money supply since the Fed can increase the monetary base, which will equal M1, as it sees fit.

Demand deposit contracts are not essential to maturity transformation, which is code for liquidity risk sharing. Charles Jacklin and others have shown that trading in securities can substitute for demand deposits. Demand deposit contracts may have some liquidity risk-sharing advantages depending on their construction in certain settings and circumstances compared to market-based insurance, but improving liquidity risk sharing in good equilibria appears to be very highly overrated relative to eliminating the risk of bad equilibria caused by fraud-based runs.[24]

The use of debt contracts to indirectly discipline bankers

who can't be monitored presupposes the bankers are bank owners, which is hardly the case, and that what bankers do can't be disclosed, and thus monitored, which it can be via the FSA.

LPB mutual funds would include credit card debt and other lines of credit, whether to households or firms. But these lines of credit would be fully funded. I.e. the mutual fund's unused lines of credit would be backed to the buck by cash holdings of the mutual fund offering the credit lines.

The FSA's disclosure of household mortgages and other debt securities would not reveal the identity of the household. For example, in the case of mortgages, the location of the house being mortgaged could be specified within a mile of its actual location, with no mention made of the borrower's name or specific employer. For households who are particularly concerned about their privacy being violated, there is an alternative available under LPB, namely to borrow from unlimited liability banks.

The FSA's disclosure of each security would include evaluations of the security's complexity and payoffs, both known and unknown, in specific states of the world. More complex securities with less well understood payoffs would be disclosed as such and, presumably, command a lower price when put up for auction. This would be for the good. Highly complex securities whose payoffs aren't well understood are like bottles of Tylenol, but with extra pills included of unknown medicinal value. Such bottles needed to be properly labelled as 'pills with unknown properties' so that people that aren't interested in random 'medical' treatments aren't induced to buy what they don't want.

In short, less may be much better than more when it comes to the number of complex securities initiated in the market place. With fewer, uniform, well-understood and fully disclosed securities, the job of the FSA will be much easier than it might seem. Also, it's important to bear in mind that information dissemination is free once that information is acquired. Hence, having the FSA evaluate and publicly disclose securities obviates the need for financial companies (each mutual fund in the case of LPB) to engage in so much duplicative security analysis.

Relationship banking doesn't disappear. Mutual fund managers will specialise in learning about particular paper issuers prior to bidding on their paper to the extent that such knowledge acquisition has value. Thus, the FSA won't preclude mutual fund managers from gathering their own private information and reaching their own judgments about the securities they might buy.

Finally, LPB permits unlimited liability banks to operate in the conventional leveraged manner. Hence, if traditional banking holds some hidden magic, unlimited liability banks will be able to capture that value. But if the unlimited liability bankers want to leverage and put the economy at risk, they will do so knowing they may lose everything they own. Switzerland, by the way, has several unlimited liability banks, which operate side-by-side with the country's large banks. But this unlimited liability financial sector is quite small compared to the limited liability financial sector and, interestingly enough, is starting to issue mutual funds to naturally limit the owners' liability.

Implementing Limited Purpose Banking

Implementing Limited Purpose Banking is straightforward. All financial corporations immediately begin marketing cash, insurance, and other mutual funds and the mutual funds start buying the FSA-processed securities at auction.

Checking account holders would be asked to sign an agreement transferring their checking account balances to cash mutual fund accounts. The government could provide a financial incentive to do this on a timely basis with all non-transferred checking account balances being remitted to their account owners at, say, the end of a year. In the US, retail banks have massive excess reserves and would have no problem covering this operation. The same appears true for the UK.

Banks would also offer their other creditors the option to transfer their credits, be they time deposits, certificates of deposits, or short, medium, and long-term bonds to mutual funds of similar longevity. Thus holders of time deposits and certificates of deposits would have their holdings of these assets transferred to short-term money market funds, which would purchase the short-term assets held by the bank.

Long-term bank creditors would be incentivised to swap their holdings for shares of mutual funds that specialize in long-term bonds, stocks or real estate. These mutual funds would then purchase these assets from the banks. In the case of real estate, the mutual funds would be closed-end funds, which don't provide for immediate redemptions, but have shares that trade in secondary markets.

This swap of debt for equity in the banking system could occur gradually over a year or two. To encourage the switch, the government could also levy taxes on bank liabilities that have not been converted to mutual fund equity after one year.

Hence, the transition to LPB is gradual with respect to unwinding existing bank assets and debts, and recycling funds out of banking and into the new more transparent financial system. But the transition is immediate with respect to issuing new mutual funds. Banks become zombies with respect to their old practices, but gazelles in exercising their new limited purpose – being the trustworthy financial intermediaries they claim to be.

5. The Commission's Reaction to Limited Purpose Banking

As indicated, the Commissioners devoted just seven sentences to rejecting Limited Purpose Banking. This is remarkable given the extremely strong, public endorsements by the likes of George Shultz, Bill Bradley, Michael Boskin, George Akerlof, Jeff Sachs, Steve Ross, Niall Ferguson, Robert Reich, Robert Lucas, Edmund Phelps, Ed Prescott, Jagdish Bhagwati, Ken Rogoff, Simon Johnson and Kevin Hassett.*

The Commission's dismissal of LPB is also surprising given the public statements made by Bank of England Governor Mervyn King endorsing analysis of Limited Purpose Banking. In September 2010, Governor King told Parliament that radical proposals for banking reform should be considered:

> I hope when your committee takes evidence from people in the US you will talk to people that have come up with pretty radical proposals, not just Paul Volcker and President Obama's team, but people like Professor Kotlikoff who have got a wider set of proposals. All of these things should be on the table for debate and discussion.[25]

And in his October 2010 Buttonwood Conference speech, Governor King stated:

> ... unless complete, capital requirements will never be able to guarantee that costs will not spill over elsewhere. This leads to the limiting case of proposals such as Professor Kotlikoff's idea to introduce what he calls 'limited purpose banking'. That would ensure that each pool of investments made by a bank is turned into a mutual fund with no maturity mismatch. There is no possibility of alchemy. It is an idea worthy of further study.[26]

---

* For example, former US Treasury Secretary and former US Secretary of State, George Shultz, in endorsing *Jimmy Stewart Is Dead*, said, 'Financial reform needs something simple, clear, and, most of all, effective. Read this book to get and understand the answer.'

In using the word alchemy, King was referring to the proposition that deposits, in particular, and bank credits, in general, can be made safe by investing in risky assets.

Finally, the Commission's treatment of Limited Purpose Banking is surprising given that one of its members, economist Martin Wolf, publicly endorsed Limited Purpose Banking in an April 27, 2010 column in the *Financial Times* entitled 'Why Cautious Reform is the Risky Option'.[27] After making the case for radical reform, Wolf turns to three alternatives: the Volcker Rule, which he endorses, but doubts can be done; John Kay's proposed version of Narrow Banking, which he thinks won't keep too-big-to-fail failures from being rescued; and Limited Purpose Banking. Here's what Wolf wrote on LPB:

> I like this idea. In essence, it says that you cannot gamble with other people's money, because, if you lose enough, the state will be forced to pay up. So, instead of having thinly capitalised entities taking risks on the lending side of the balance sheet while promising to redeem fixed obligations, financial institutions would become mutual funds. Risk would then be clearly and explicitly borne by households, who own all the equity, anyway. In this world, financial intermediaries would not pretend to be able to meet obligations that, in many states of the world, they simply cannot.

Presumably, Wolf's voice and views got drowned out by the other Commission members, for here is all they said about LPB in the report:

> Limited purpose banking offers an alternative solution, under which the role of financial intermediaries is to bring together savers and borrowers but risk is eliminated from the intermediary because it does not hold the loan on its books. All of the risk of the loan is passed onto the investors in the intermediary (or fund), so that effectively all debt is securitised. However, limited purpose banking would severely constrain two key functions of the financial system. First, it would constrain banks' ability to produce liquidity through the creation of liabilities (deposits) with shorter maturities than their assets. The existence of such deposits allows households and firms to settle payments easily. Second, banks would no longer be

incentivised to monitor their borrowers, and it would be more difficult to modify loan agreements. These activities help to maximise the economic value of bank loans.[28]

Of the seven sentences, only four contain substantive criticisms. The other three describe the proposal. And each of the criticisms is very far off-base.

Take the report's statement that LPB 'would constrain banks' ability to produce liquidity through the creation of liabilities (deposits) with shorter maturities than their assets. The existence of such deposits allows households and firms to settle payments easily.'

This statement is astonishing on several fronts.

First, if the report is referring to liquidity as M1, it should know that the size of M1 is, in the end, what the central bank wants it to be, not what banks decide it should be, i.e. the central bank can offset changes in the M1 money multiplier by increasing the monetary base to the extent desired. In recent years, as M1 money multipliers plunged, the Federal Reserve, the Bank of England and the European Central Bank have expanded M1 by dramatically increasing the size of their monetary bases.

Second, the essence of a liquid asset is that it can be quickly exchanged for goods and services at reliable terms of trade. Short-term liabilities are safe and liquid right up to the point that they aren't – when the run is on. The banking system cannot create true, lasting liquidity via what Governor King calls 'alchemy'. It can only create the illusion of such liquidity.

Third, while LPB shuts down the alchemists, fractional reserve bankers, it certainly doesn't constrain banks' ability to produce liquidity. On the contrary, it includes cash mutual funds, whose size relative to the economy can be as large as the central bank desires and which are always liquid because they are always fully backed pound for pound. Under LPB, the money multiplier is always 1 so the central bank has full control of M1 at all times. Constraining the banks to keep the money multiplier at 1 actually means they can't reduce it when they panic. So LPB is not constraining banks' ability to produce liquidity. It's constraining banks' ability to reduce liquidity.

Fourth, cash mutual funds would *always* permit settlement of payments, which cannot be said of the current system. Again, when the report makes statements like: 'The existence of … deposits allows households and firms to settle payments easily', it is talking about non-crisis conditions. In conditions of financial crisis, marked by runs, the existence of short-term deposits transformed into long-term assets that can suddenly lose value does precisely the opposite. It makes the system unstable and provokes a run, which destroys liquidity. There is ample evidence of this in the eurozone today and plenty of terrible examples in 2007 and 2008.

Fifth, under LPB, all mutual fund shares, whether closed-end or open-end, trade in the market and should be highly liquid given the on-going, online disclosure by the FSA of the mutual fund holdings. Moreover, liquidity is enhanced not just by transparency, but by simplicity. Complex securities are hard to understand and, thus, hard to trade. By enforcing the auctioning of all financial securities purchased and sold by mutual funds, LPB will naturally lead to fewer and less complex financial securities.

Sixth, the use of fractional reserve banking in which depositors are promised their money back on demand is not essential for liquidity risk sharing. Recall my previous mention of Jacklin's more than two-decades-old research on this subject showing that the holding short- and long-date securities can share liquidity risk without the danger of a bank run. Indeed, in states of the world with bank runs, the Diamond-Dybvig model of banking – the one we have and the Commission wants to keep – destroys liquidity risk sharing. Stated differently, it produces liquidity risk as well as liquidity insurance depending on the states of nature involved because, in times of bank runs, agents who have sudden demands for liquidity end up, potentially, losing all their assets.

It's perhaps worth mentioning that I made each of these six points in meeting privately with the Commission for over two hours in February of 2011.

The Commission's other stated concern with LPB is that 'banks would no longer be incentivised to monitor their borrowers and would find it more difficult to modify loan agreements'.

I disagree. Under LPB, the banks are mutual funds and the mutual funds that buy loans will be run by managers (LPB bankers) who will have very strong incentives to keep track of their creditors. If they see their creditors getting into trouble, they will do better in terms of their funds' return performance by selling the loans (in the case of open end funds) in question or by bidding less for new bonds issued by their creditors looking to refinance. And mutual fund managers will get paid on one basis and one basis only, their fund's return performance. In contrast, in the current banking system, banker compensation is tied, it seems, not to a clear metric of performance, but to one's friends on the compensation committee. How else would one explain the enormous payouts to bankers who destroyed their firms?

Another key difference under LPB is that the FSA will be continually monitoring the condition of loans. If Fred Bloggs, who borrowed £100,000 to buy a house in Middlesborough, loses his job, that fact will be duly disclosed in real time on the web so that no mutual fund holding Fred's loan can fraudulently convey that loan to an innocent buyer at auction.

The US financial system just collapsed, in large part, because of the failure to monitor the initiation of mortgages. It's truly astounding that the Commission, which puts nothing in place to monitor independently security initiation – the area where monitoring is most critical, is concerned about LPB in this regard. It's as if the Commission entirely ignored the role of risk regulation, although I explained the new role of the FSA at length in my meeting with the Commission.

The Commission appears to be ignoring the colossal failure to monitor security initiations while blithely assuming that this behaviour won't arise again because shareholders, creditors and regulators will suddenly begin to monitor the bankers to make sure they do their due diligence. This is sheer fantasy.

As for the issue of having their loans modified when they can't repay, we've seen that under the current system this is not exactly a matter of calling up one's local banker and saying: 'Gee, my wife just broke her ankle, I've got a big bill from the dentist for little Billy, and some other pressing problems right now, so, how about we reduce the loan that I owe you?' For one thing, one's local banker these days is a clerk for some huge national, if not multinational bank and the process is pretty straightforward – 'either pay or we foreclose'. Governments have been strenuously fostering loan modifications, but the fact that they've had to do so and achieved such meagre results is testimony to the enormous moral hazard associated with such procedures.

This said, to the extent that the market begins to issue mortgages with automatic loan modification provisions, they could just as well be purchased by mutual funds as by traditional banks. And to the extent that standard mortgages remain the norm, in which modification is made by creditors on an ad-hoc basis, there is no reason that mutual funds holding such mortgages would be less willing to make such changes to non-performing loans than today's banks.

Indeed, there is a very important respect in which LPB permits modifications of mortgages and loans, in general, to proceed much more readily. Under LPB, mortgages and other loans will be held in whole, not in slices, by the mutual funds. Under LPB, mutual funds are, themselves, securitisations that entail diversified holdings of particular types of assets. The mutual funds would be required to hold the original title to the securities they buy and could not promise to pay some income from their securities to individuals who are not their shareholders because such an arrangement would constitute borrowing, which is prohibited.

Mind you, within a closed-end mortgage mutual fund, particular equity investors could sign up for less risk and more sure income than other equity investors; i.e. the mutual fund itself could constitute a collateralised mortgage obligation or a collateralized debt obligation. But in all cases, the underlying securities would be held by the mutual fund in their entirety, which would make modification possible in many instances where that's currently not the case.

Specific concerns with the commission's proposals

Before concluding this critique of the Vickers Report, let me focus on some of its implementation details that give me pause.

My first concern is with the operation of ringfenced banks within larger banking groups. According to the report, the majority of the ringfenced bank directors as well as the chairmen of the boards of these banks, are to be independent directors. This means that these independent directors, rather than the directors of the banking group, will have the ultimate say over the actions of the ringfenced banks, which the banking group owns.

The Commission's goal here is to maintain banking synergies, with the ringfenced retail banks sharing physical space, technology and, presumably, marketing, accounting and other operations. But the clear trouble with this scheme is that the banking group and the ringfenced banks may not see eye to eye on lots of issues, including resource sharing. Furthermore, the ringfenced bank may feel it owes primary allegiance to the public, not to the shareholders of the banking group.

The sharing of resources also makes it likely that letting the larger banking group fail will impose bankruptcy costs on its ringfenced banking group as well. If, for example, both the larger banking group and ringfenced banking group share space, information systems and the use of in-house marketing personnel, what happens if the larger banking group fails? Does the ringfenced bank need to vacate the premises, which are now owned by the creditors who may want to sell the building? Does the ringfenced bank continue to get access to the same information technology, which was owned, in larger part, by the larger banking group? Will the marketing team still be available if most of its *raison d' être* is no more?

What happens if the ringfenced bank and larger banking group differ on strategy, location, or a host of other issues? Can the ringfenced bank go its own way and force the larger banking group to live with its decisions or be forced to sell the operation? For example, if the ringfenced bank wants to move into separate, and very expensive premises, leaving the banking group with unutilized space, is that acceptable?

'Leave it to the regulators'

A second major concern is the leeway regulators are given by the Commission in implementing the new banking policy. For example, in the case of the appointment of independent bankers, the report says this should 'normally' occur. But what are normal circumstances and what are abnormal circumstances are not defined. This leaves unclear who will ultimately be in charge of roughly one third of the UK banking system.

Another example of 'leave it to the regulators' is the leeway given with respect to the amount and nature of loss-absorbing debt. The report says that total primary loss-absorbing capacity should be 17 per cent to 20 per cent of risk-weighted assets, with regulators deciding what precise figure is appropriate based on the risk to the taxpayer.

A third example is the mix of the loss-absorbing debt as between contingent capital and bail-in bonds. Collectively, these two forms of debt are supposed to equal from 7 to 10 per cent of risk-weighted assets. And the contingent capital is designed to kick in before resolution and bail-in bonds are supposed to activate in resolution. The Commission leaves it up to the regulators and to the bankers, themselves, as to what mix to adopt. It also leaves it up to the regulators how to define bail-in bonds, when to impose losses on bail-in bonds, whether to impose write-downs on these bonds or force debt-to-equity conversions, and what fraction of the 'long-term' (which, actually, is as short-term as one year) bail-in bonds is to be of particular maturities.

A fourth example is the power of regulators to restrict dividend payments and bonuses of banks whose loss-absorbing capacity falls below the Commission's proposed minimum thresholds.

A fifth example is the discretion of regulators in deciding what criteria should influence their decision on moving the 17 per cent loss-absorbing minimum to as high as 20 per cent. In this regard, the Commission lets regulators consider 'the complexity of a bank's structure and activities', 'the availability and likely effectiveness of available resolution tools for reducing the impact of a bank's failure', 'any evidence that a bank is benefiting from an implicit government guarantee', and 'a bank's contribution to systemic risk, its resolvability and the level of risk posed to the UK taxpayer in resolution'.

A sixth example is the potential for taxpayer bailouts. The report states:

> The recommendations would sharpen incentives for monitoring and market discipline by removing a cushion from the downside that comes from the possibility that government will step in to bail out banks while keeping creditors largely whole. The ability both to separate out the functions where continuous provision is vital for the economy and to distribute losses appropriately among shareholders and creditors would have this effect and so curtail the implicit guarantee.

This statement says two mutually exclusive things: that the Commission is both 'removing' the possibility of bailouts and that it is 'curtailing' the possibility of bailouts. In using such convoluted, ambiguous and contradictory language, the Commission is admitting that bailouts are, in fact, possible. But it leaves it to the regulators to decide when.

A seventh example is the leeway the Commission leaves regulators to change the rules of the game through time.

The problem with providing regulators with so much discretion is that purchasers of bank stock and bank bonds, whether they are the securities of 'good' or 'bad' banks, will have even less idea of what they are buying under the Commission's reforms than is the case today. Indeed, unless the conditions under which contingent capital is activated and bail-in bonds are bailed in and the degrees to which the activations and bail-ins occur are made precise, there may be no one willing to buy these securities.

In this case, the Commission will have succeeded in eliminating much of bank funding because it states clearly that *all* unsecured debt with a maturity of greater than one year must be bail-inable.

So why did the Commission leave regulators so much leeway to micromanage the banking system potentially to death? Why didn't it make crystal clear how ringfenced banks would interact with their parents, or stipulate the precise kind of contingent capital and bail-in bonds to be issued, or specify the exact criteria under which the regulators would require more loss-absorbing capital?

The answer is that the commissioners don't have answers to any of these questions because there are no clear answers to be had. Instead, the Commission passed the ball to the regulators and let it be a matter of regulatory discretion. This leaves banks, bankers and the bank securities market with considerably more uncertainty about future banking rules.

For the households and non-financial firms using the banking system, this takes opacity to an even higher level. Not only are these bank customers left in the dark as to what the banks are doing with their money. They are also left in the dark about what the regulators will be doing with the banks.

And pity the poor regulators who need to make rulings based on highly opaque data in settings where the banks could easily get into terrible trouble while obeying all the rules. These regulators are being told by the Commission to play it tough at a time when the economy may be in grave danger and the state of animal spirits is ready to crack.

Conclusion

The Vickers Commission set out to make banking safe, to ensure that what just happened won't happen again, and to change both the structure and regulation of banking as needed. Unfortunately, the Commission was more concerned about the boat than keeping it off the rocks. As a result, it ended up doing far too little at a cost that is far too high.

A clear path to a safe financial system and a safe economy – Limited Purpose Banking – lay before this distinguished group of academics and financial practitioners. But they opted to gamble with High Street to placate Lombard Street. Had they left the system in its current sorry state, their failure would have been bad enough. But they have arguably made the financial system worse. Rather than focus on the two principal causes of the developed world's financial crisis – opacity and leverage – they set about to 'fix' things that weren't broken and had nothing to do with the crisis past or the crisis to come.

The payment system, proprietary trading by retail banks, and derivative trading by retail banks had as much to do with the fundamental causes of the banking crisis as Iraq had to do with 9/11. But fixing these things and pretending that big bad banks will be allowed to fail, when the Commission can't even say so in plain English, is the main motivation for ringfencing retail banking. Ironically, to the extent that the customers of the bad banks believe the pretence is real, they will run much more quickly than they just did and force the government to engage in even larger bailouts than would otherwise occur.

The other key element of the 'reform' is new prudential regulation. This consists of three things: a slightly higher ratio of capital to risk-weighted assets than Basel III mandates, but that remains below the capital ratio Lehman had right before its collapse; an acceptance of Basel III's ridiculously high 33 to 1 permissible leverage ratio, which is also much higher than Lehman's ratio when it collapsed; and the requirement of speedy bank funerals via loss-absorbing debt, whose issuance may be impossible given the uncertainties associated with its payoff.

The Commission's proposals are a full employment act for regulators and a nightmare in the making for bankers. A banking system that was terribly risky will, on balance, end up riskier, a regulatory system that was dysfunctional will now have many more things to get wrong, and a population that was praying for a sure economic future will be left on its knees.

Figure 2.1 Euro Area Sovereign Bond Spreads over the Benchmark German Bunds

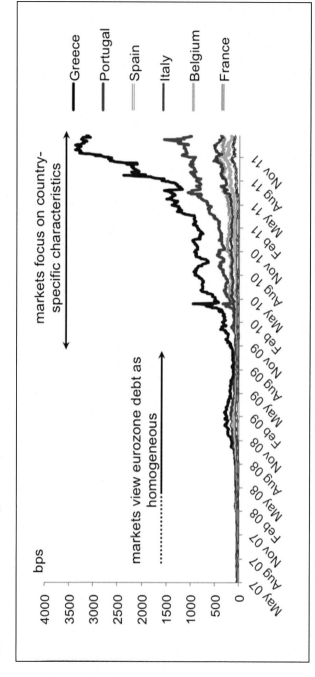

Source: Mansoor Dailami, 'Looking Beyond the Developed World's Sovereign Debt Crisis,' The World Bank, Economic Premise, No. 76, March 2012.

Figure 2.2 *European Sovereign and Bank Credit Rating Changes, January 2008–January 2012 (Italy, Belgium, Portugal)*

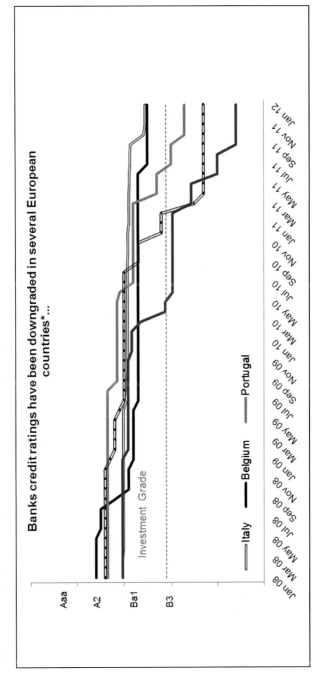

Banks credit ratings have been downgraded in several European countries*...

Source: Mansoor Dailami, 'Looking Beyond the Developed World's Sovereign Debt Crisis,' The World Bank, Economic Premise, No. 76, March 2012.

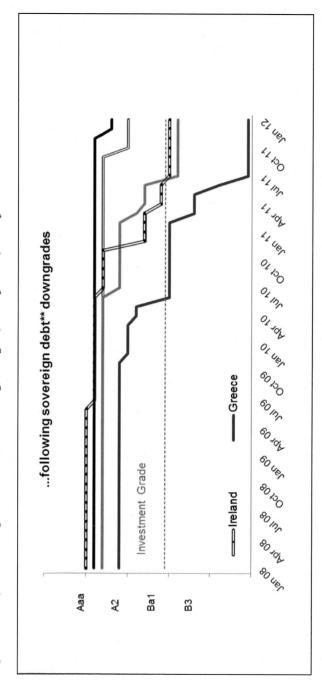

Figure 2.3 European Sovereign and Bank Credit Rating Changes, January 2008–January 2012 (Ireland and Greece)

Source: Mansoor Dailami, 'Looking Beyond the Developed World's Sovereign Debt Crisis,' The World Bank, Economic Premise, No. 76, March 2012.

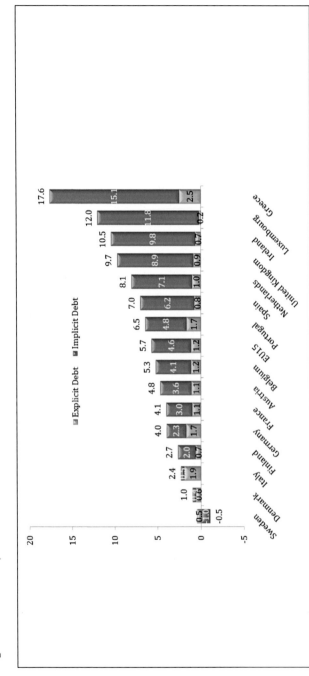

Figure 3.1: Fiscal Gap in UK and Other EU Countries as Percentage of Present Value of GDP, 2010

Source: Bernd Raffelhüschen and Stefen Moog, Research Center for Generational Contracts, University of Freiburg, calculations based on European Commission data.

Figure 3.2 European Bank's Exposure to Domestic and Foreign Sovereign Debt

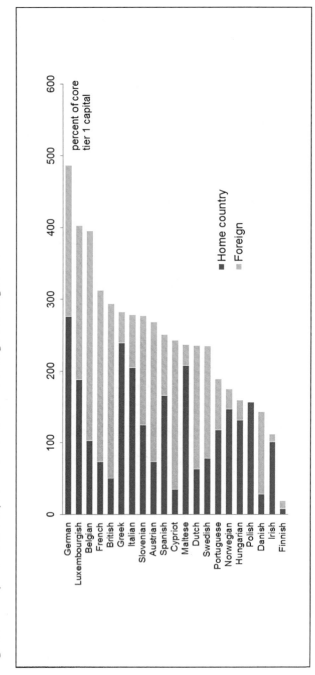

Source: Mansoor Dailami, 'Looking Beyond the Developed World's Sovereign Debt Crisis,' The World Bank, Economic Premise, No. 76, March 2012.

Notes

1   'UK unemployment continues to edge up', *BBC News*, 15 February
     2012: http://www.bbc.co.uk/news/business-17039513
2   'Interim Report', *Independent Commission on Banking*, April 2011:
     http://www.hm-treasury.gov.uk/d/icb_interim_report_full_
     document.pdf
3   Kirkup, James, 'World facing worst financial crisis in history, Bank
     of England Governor says', *Daily Telegraph*, 6 October 2011:
     http://www.telegraph.co.uk/finance/financialcrisis/8812260/
     World-facing-worst-financial-crisis-in-history-Bank-of-England-
     Governor-says.html
4   'Finance crisis: In graphics', *BBC News*, 3 November 2008:
     http://news.bbc.co.uk/2/hi/business/7644238.stm
5   King, Mervyn, 'Banking: From Bagehot to Basel, and Back Again',
     The Second Bagehot Lecture, *Buttonwood Gathering*, New York City,
     Monday 25 October 2010: http://www.bankofengland.co.uk/
     publications/Documents/speeches/2010/speech455.pdf
6   See Kotlikoff, Laurence J., *Jimmy Stewart Is Dead*, New York, NY:
     John Wiley & Sons, 2010.
7   'The Bank that failed', *The Economist*, 20 September 2007:
     http://www.economist.com/node/9832838
8   Diamond, Peter A., 'Aggregate Demand Management in Search
     Equilibrium', *Journal of Political Economy*, 90(5), 881-894, 1982.
9   Source: 'United States Business Confidence' and 'United Kingdom
     Business Confidence', *tradingeconomics.com*:
     http://www.tradingeconomics.com/united-states/business-
     confidence; http://www.tradingeconomics.com/united-
     kingdom/business-confidence
10   Dailami, Mansoor. 'Looking Beyond the Developed World's
     Sovereign Debt Crisis', *World Bank*, Economic Premise, No. 76,
     March 2012.
11   *Final Report* (Vickers Report), Independent Commission on
     Banking, p. 16: http://bankingcommission.s3.amazonaws.com/
     wp-content/uploads/2010/07/ICB-Final-Report.pdf
12   'IMF Downgrades Britain's Economic Growth Forecast', *Huffington
     Post*, 24 January 2012: http://www.huffingtonpost.co.uk/2012/
     01/24/imf-britain-growth-forecast-economic-recession_n_
     1227691.html?just_reloaded=1
13   See Green, Jerry and Laurence J. Kotlikoff, 'On the General
     Relativity of Fiscal Policy', in Alan J. Auerbach and Daniel Shaviro,
     eds., *Key Issues in Public Finance – A Conference in Memory of David
     Bradford*, Harvard University Press, 2009: http://www.kotlikoff.
     net/content/general-relativity-fiscal-language.

14   Speakes, Jeff, 'Goodhart's Law and Basel', *Center for Economic Research and Forecasting*, 21 December 2011: http://www.clucerf. org/blog/2011/12/21/goodharts-law-and-basel/
15   Prepared Testimony of Richard S. Fuld, Jr., *ABC News*, 6 October 2008: http://abcnews.go.com/Business/story?id=5963581 &page=4#.T10LbZeXTyc
16   See: 'Capital Adequacy Review', Lehman Brothers, 11 September 2008: http://www.jenner.com/lehman/docs/debtors/LBEX-DOCID%20012124.pdf
17   'Statement of Richard S. Fuld, Jr. before the United States House of Representatives Committee on Financial Services', *United States House of Representatives*,20 April 2010: http://www.house.gov/ apps/list/hearing/financialsvcs_dem/fuld_4.20.10.pdf
18   'Lehman bankruptcy payout plan gains momentum', *Thomson Reuters*, 29 September 2011: http://newsandinsight. thomsonreuters.com/Bankruptcy/News/2011/09_-_September/ Lehman_bankruptcy_payout_plan_gains_momentum/
19   Sloan, Allan, 'Surprise! The big bad bailout is paying off', CNN, 8 July 2011: http://finance.fortune.cnn.com/tag/lehman-brothers/
20   Vickers Report, p.7.
21   These companies could be the current rating companies, e.g., Moody's and Standard & Poors, provided they worked strictly for the FSA.
22   'Trends in Mutual Fund Investing', Investment Company Institute, March 2012: http://www.ici.org/research/stats/trends/ trends_03_12
23   Shiller, Robert J., *Finance and the Good Society*, Princeton University Press, 2012.
24   Jacklin, Charles, 'Demand Deposits, Trading Restrictions, and Risk-Sharing,' in E Prescott and N Wallace (eds), *Contractual Arrangements for Intertemporal Trade*, University of Minnesota Press, 1987.
25   Ryan, Jennifer and O'Donnell, Svenja, 'King Says "Radical" Proposals Like Obama's Needed for Banking', Bloomberg, 26 January 2010: http://www.bloomberg.com/apps/news?pid =newsarchive&sid=abzJpJPoCD6s
26   King, Mervyn, 'Banking: From Bagehot to Basel, and Back Again', The Second Bagehot Lecture, *Buttonwood Gathering*, New York City, Monday 25 October 2010: http://www.bankofengland.co.uk/ publications/Documents/speeches/2010/speech455.pdf
27   Wolf, Martin, 'Why cautious reform is the risky option', *Financial Times*, 27 April 2010: http://www.ft.com/intl/cms/s/0/cca02e40-522d-11df-8b09-00144feab49a.html#axzz1pOGXMNf2
28   Vickers Report p. 44.